ATLANTIS

Herbie Brennan is a professional writer whose work has appeared in more than fifty countries. He began a career in journalism at the age of eighteen and when he was twenty-four became the youngest newspaper editor in his native Ireland.

By his mid-twenties, he had published his first novel, an historical romance brought out by Doubleday in New York. At age thirty, he made the decision to devote his time to full-length works of fiction for both adults and children. Since then he has published more than one hundred books, many of them international bestsellers, for both adults and children.

Other books by Herbie Brennan
published by Faber & Faber

Space Quest
111 peculiar questions about the universe and beyond

The Spy's Handbook

The Ghosthunter's Handbook

The Aliens Handbook

HERBIE BRENNAN'S FORBIDDEN TRUTHS
ATLANTIS

Herbie Brennan

Illustrated by The Maltings Partnership

faber and faber

Illustrated by The Maltings Partnership

First published in 2006 by Faber and Faber Limited
3 Queen Square, London WC1N 3AU

Layout and typesetting by Andy Summers: Planet Creative Ltd

Project Management: Paula Borton

Printed in England by Bookmarque Ltd

All rights reserved

© Herbie Brennan, 2006

Herbie Brennan is hereby identified as author of this work in accordance with Section 77 of the Copyright, Designs and Patents Act 1988

This book is sold subject to the condition that it shall not, by way of trade or otherwise, be lent, resold, hired out or otherwise circulated without the publisher's prior consent in any form of binding or cover other than that in which it is published and without a similar condition including this condition being imposed on the subsequent purchaser

A CIP record for this book is available from the British Library

The website addresses (URLs) included in this book were valid at the time of going to press. However, because of the nature of the Internet it is possible that some sites may have closed down or changed. While the author and publisher regret any inconvenience, no responsibility can be accepted for such changes.

ISBN 978-0-571-22313-8
ISBN 0-571-22313-3

2 4 6 8 10 9 7 5 3

CONTENTS

CHAPTER 1	Cosmic catastrophe	9
CHAPTER 2	Prehistoric timeline	11
CHAPTER 3	Forbidden facts about humanity	13
CHAPTER 4	Forbidden facts about prehistory	16
CHAPTER 5	What happens to forbidden facts?	18
CHAPTER 6	The big freeze	21
CHAPTER 7	Civilisation	24
CHAPTER 8	Lost civilisation	27
CHAPTER 9	Cataclysm Atlantis	30
CHAPTER 10	Land of gold	35
CHAPTER 11	Royal hunt	40
CHAPTER 12	Where was Atlantis?	44
CHAPTER 13	Ice Age theory	48
CHAPTER 14	Causes of the Ice Age	52
CHAPTER 15	Forbidden facts about the Ice Age	56
CHAPTER 16	Big mistakes	60
CHAPTER 17	Impossible Atlantis	64
CHAPTER 18	Forbidden facts about early writing	69
CHAPTER 19	Forbidden facts about prehistoric art	74
CHAPTER 20	A museum of forbidden facts	79
CHAPTER 21	Stone movers of the Ancient World	87
CHAPTER 22	Stone moving without tears	94
CHAPTER 23	Prehistoric city	101
CHAPTER 24	More prehistoric cities	108
CHAPTER 25	Prehistoric engineering	115
CHAPTER 26	Prehistoric navigators	121
CHAPTER 27	Marvellous maps	127
CHAPTER 28	Prehistoric civilisation	134
CHAPTER 29	Ancient pyramids	137
CHAPTER 30	Mexican mystery	141
CHAPTER 31	Memories of Atlantis	149
CHAPTER 32	Lost Lemuria	155
CHAPTER 33	Evidence for Lemuria	163
CHAPTER 34	The death of Atlantis	169
CHAPTER 35	The shifting Earth	178
CHAPTER 36	The falling sky	183
CHAPTER 37	The aftermath	191

For Dolores, with love
and fond memories of Atlantis

ATLANTIS

What if...
    ... you can't trust your teachers? What if you can't believe your parents?

What if...
    ... the things you know for sure are just plain wrong?

What if...
    ... scientists sometimes just make up the answers?

What if...
    ... the world is not the way you think it is? What if history is all lies? What if the stuff they tell you is impossible keeps happening every day?

ATLANTIS

What if...
... time travel is already happening ... parallel worlds are real ... you have powers beyond your wildest dreams?

What if...
... Atlantis once existed?

Chapter 1
COSMIC CATASTROPHE

There's something wrong with our solar system. All the pictures you've ever seen show the planets orbiting the sun like clockwork, but actually they don't. Astronomically speaking, the whole thing is a wreck. Planetary orbits and positions aren't what they should be.

✩ Pluto looks as if it may once have been a moon of Neptune.

✩ Uranus spins too fast and is tilted to one side.

✩ There's an area beyond Pluto that could be the remains of an exploded planet.

✩ Some astronomers even believe the asteroid belt between Mars and Jupiter might be the remains of an exploded planet as well.

ATLANTIS

Experts believe something very large and nasty visited us once, disrupting everything in its path... including Planet Earth. The textbooks say all this occurred 'several million years ago.' But that's just guesswork. Our solar system might as easily have been wrecked several *thousand* years ago.

And if it was, then there were human beings who watched it happen. There were human beings who suffered and died when the intruder passed too close to Earth.

Chapter 2
PREHISTORIC TIMELINE

According to the fossil record, the story of humanity began with creatures called *hominids*, a group that split off from African apes about six million years ago.

One or two million years later, some of these *hominids* developed into what are now called *Australopithecines*. The *pithecine* part of *Australopithecine* means we're talking about apes, but these were apes with a difference. They sometimes walked upright and they used stones and bones as simple tools.

Australopithecines gave rise to *Homo habilis* ('Handy

Homo habilis

ATLANTIS

Man') the very first being on our planet ever to make tools. *Australopithecines* used things they happened to find as tools, but *Habilis* was the first actually to make them.

Scientists believe *Homo habilis* evolved into early brutish humans given the name of *Homo erectus* ('Upright Man') who walked on his hind legs all the time, hunted in packs and eventually got around to using fire.

In another couple of million years, evolution had given us *Homo sapiens* ('Wise Man') and his squat, beetle-browed cousin, *Homo Neanderthalensis* ('Neanderthal Man'). Finally, a little over 100,000 years ago our own species, *Homo sapiens sapiens* ('Wise, Wise Man') appeared on the scene.

Which means that if the cosmic catastrophe occurred at any time since then, our own ancestors were there to see it. But they were, of course, too primitive to leave us any record of the disastrous event.

Or were they?

Homo erectus

Homo sapiens sapiens

Chapter 3

FORBIDDEN FACTS ABOUT HUMANITY

What you've just read is the story your teachers will tell you if you ask them where the human race came from. It's the same story you'll read in your textbooks and encyclopedias, the same story you'll watch dramatised in television documentaries, the same story you'll see spelled out in museum displays. There's only one thing wrong with it – it isn't true.

The story of humanity that's put forward with such confidence is based on a tiny amount of hard evidence ... almost all of which is disputed by some expert or another. Here are a few facts:

 The remains from which we've figured out the history of billions of human ancestors over millions of years wouldn't fill the back

ATLANTIS

of a small truck. Most of them are nothing more than tiny slivers of bone.

- Some scientists originally thought the distinctive brow ridges of Neanderthal Man were caused by too much frowning.

- If you put together every *Homo erectus* specimen we've ever discovered, they'd fit into your school bus with room left over for the driver.

- The entire history of *Homo habilis* has been worked out from two incomplete skeletons and a few limb bones. These appear to show the males of the species were growing more human while the females were getting more apelike.

- Humanity shares the first 99.99999% of its early history with chimpanzees.

- We know nothing at all about the prehistory of chimpanzees.

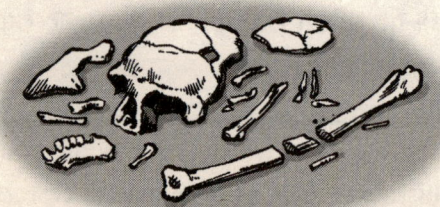

That picture in your textbooks illustrating the evolution of humans – the one where the shambling ape gets more and more upright and human looking – is pure fiction. Almost every detail from skin colouring, hairiness, muscle tone, posture, facial expression to types of nose are the result of somebody's imagination.

Those things show that what you're being taught about the evolution of humanity is based on very shaky foundations. What comes next shows most of it is nonsense.

Chapter 4
FORBIDDEN FACTS ABOUT PREHISTORY

A human skull fragment found in Hungary has been dated between 250,000 and 450,000 BC. A human footprint discovered in France along with stone and bone tools, hearths and shelters was dated 300,000 to 400,000 years BC.

Other French finds include a partial human skeleton and a human jawbone that are at least 300,000 years old. So are two English skeletons found at Ipswich and Galley Hill, just north of London; the Ipswich skeleton may be as much as 600,000 years old. Hearths, charcoal, human thigh bones and broken animal bones, all pointing towards the existence of modern humanity, were discovered in Java. Their date is 830000 BC.

These finds show modern humanity was in Europe and Asia anything between 150,000 to 730,000 years before we were even supposed to have evolved in Africa. It gets worse. A human skeleton discovered at Midi in France, stone tools found in Portugal, Burma and Argentina, a carved bone and flint flakes from Turkey all have a minimum age of 5 *million* years. That means people like you and I were about at the time the very first *Australopithecines* were appearing in Africa.

Human bones from Placer County, in California, are known to be older than 8.7 million years. There are various stone tools, a stone bead, a human jaw and skull fragment, some spear heads, and several ladles – all Californian – that have a minimum dating of 9 million BC ... that's a whole 3,000,000 years before our ancestral *hominids* were supposed to split off from the prehistoric apes of Africa.

A human skeleton was unearthed in Switzerland with an estimated age of between 38 and 45 million years. In France there were stone tools, cut wood and even a carved chalk ball, the *minimum* ages of which range from 45 to 50 million years. There are even finds – which I'll go into in more detail later – that suggest our ancestors invented writing, mined metal and, incredibly, built cities in the far depths of prehistory.

These discoveries – and there are thousands more like them – show that what you've been taught about the course of human evolution is contradicted by some very solid (but forbidden) facts.

Chapter 5

WHAT HAPPENS TO FORBIDDEN FACTS?

What happens when you turn up a forbidden fact is actually quite creepy. Take the case of Dr Thomas E. Lee, who worked for the National Museum of Canada.

In the early 1950s, Lee discovered stone tools on an island in Lake Huron. An expert from Wayne State University dated them at least 65,000 years old – and thought there was a good possibility that they might be nearly twice that age. The problem was that the textbooks claimed there were no human beings in the Americas before 12,000 BC, when they crossed over from Europe by way of a now-submerged land bridge into Alaska.

If you look it up, you'll find that's what the textbooks *still* say. So what happened to Dr Lee and his finds?

WHAT HAPPENS TO FORBIDDEN FACTS?

According to Lee himself, he was, hounded from his civil service position into unemployment; nobody would publish his works; the evidence was misrepresented by several prominent authors; tonnes of artefacts vanished into storage bins of the National Museum of Canada.

And it didn't stop there. When Lee's boss refused to fire him and proposed publishing a paper on the finds, he was fired in his turn. Lee's opponents tried to grab the only six of his finds that hadn't already been hidden away. Then the site of his discoveries was turned into a tourist resort, making sure nobody would dig up any more embarrassing specimens.

You might imagine that what happened to Dr Lee was an isolated case. But try telling that to the geologist Virginia Steen-McIntyre. Back in 1973, she was rash enough to put a date of 250,000 BC on some advanced stone tools found in Mexico. This not only contradicted the textbook claim of when humans first reached South America, it also contradicted the textbook claim that the earliest humans capable of making such tools only evolved in Africa 150,000 years later.

But as you may have noticed, they didn't change the textbooks. Instead they tried to stop Dr Steen-McIntyre publishing her findings. When the findings did eventually come out, archaeologists simply rejected or ignored them. Dr Steen-McIntyre later commented,

ATLANTIS

"I didn't realise ... how deeply woven into our thought the current theory of human evolution had become. Our work ... has been rejected by most archaeologists because it contradicts that theory..!"

Fiddling with the facts has been a favourite occupation of scientists for a very long time. Way back in 1880, the State Geologist of California published a review of advanced stone implements – including pestles and mortars – found in local gold mines at a level that would make them somewhere between 9 million and 55 million years old. These astounding discoveries didn't make anybody rewrite the textbooks either.

If the facts don't fit the theory, you should throw away the facts.

Chapter 6

THE BIG FREEZE

Whatever problems there may be about the textbook view of early humans, the scientists are certain they've got the first civilisation absolutely taped. It came about, they say, to celebrate the ending of the Ice Age.

The start of the last Ice Age was some 1,600,000 years ago. More than 45 million square kilometres (27,963,000 miles) of our planet's landmass disappeared under glaciers and ice sheets – something like 30% of the entire globe. (Only about 10% is glaciated today, and most of that is on high mountain ranges.) Parts of the northern oceans were either frozen over or had extensive ice shelves.

Canada was covered by a network of glaciers so large that it might as well have been a continuous blanket of ice. In the United States, New York City, Cincinnati, St. Louis and Kansas City were all buried

ATLANTIS

under ice – or would have been if they'd existed then. There were ice valleys in Hawaii. Greenland and Iceland were almost entirely ice covered.

Nearly half of Europe went under the Scandinavian Ice Sheet. It covered most of Britain and extended south across central Germany, then Poland, before creeping northeast over the northern Russian Plain to the Arctic Ocean. Much of Siberia groaned under mountain glaciers while the Siberian Ice Sheet covered its northwestern plain. The Alps, the Caucasus, and the Pyrenees all carried monstrous glaciers.

THE BIG FREEZE

In the Southern Hemisphere, there were ice caps and glaciers in Mexico and Central America. Existing glaciers in the Andes spread westward into Chile and eastward onto the pampas of Argentina. Mountains in Japan and New Guinea supported valley glaciers. New glaciers developed in New Zealand and on mountains in Africa and Tasmania, including some located on the Equator. Antarctica had even more ice than it has today. Global temperatures dropped by 5°C or more. The world was in deep freeze.

Chapter 7

CIVILISATION

As you've already seen, scientists insist (despite certain evidence to the contrary) that modern humanity began to move out of Africa into this chill, hostile world somewhere around 100,000 years ago.

It's difficult to figure what could have coaxed our ancestors out of their warm, well-fed home. But something did and once they left the rainforest, their only chance of survival lay in following the great migrating herds or foraging for any other food that might be growing wild. They wrapped themselves in furs, shivered in caves – later in primitive, semi-portable shelters – and lived as nomads (people who have no permanent home) until they died.

The Ice Age finally ended around 8000 BC when the Scandinavian ice sheet broke up. Before that happened, one or two groups of hunter-gatherers

CIVILISATION

more or less tamed their own little herds of reindeer and kept them the way we now keep cattle. Then, as temperatures began to rise, humankind took to farming in a big way.

Farming provided more food for more people. Population numbers increased and nearly everybody started to live in permanent settlements. By the seventh millennium BC, there were villages scattered across the Middle East. Some of them even bartered goods with one another, laying the foundations of trade.

Then, around 3300 BC, the Sumerians, who probably came from Anatolia in what's now Turkey, moved into the southernmost part of Mesopotamia (now modern Iraq), and started to establish city states. By the third

CIVILISATION

millennium BC there were at least a dozen of them. These cities, surrounded by farmland, became the first civilisation. Other civilisations followed in Egypt, Assyria, Greece and Rome.

If you take the scientific picture as a whole, it was one long, slow, cold, straight-line march from the grunting cave man to the city slicker.

That's if you still believe the scientific picture. A man named Solon believed something very different. Something that might tie in with the near destruction of our solar system.

Chapter 8

LOST CIVILISATION

Solon was born in 630 BC and became famous as a politician and poet. When the political situation in his native Athens led to the brink of civil war, he was asked to bring in new laws to stop the crisis. Solon's laws were one of the great achievements of Ancient Greece, but he got no thanks for them at the time. After begging for change, nobody really wanted it. The poor complained he hadn't done enough, the rich that he'd done far too much.

Solon couldn't be bothered to argue. He told everybody to get on with it, announced he was leaving Greece and pledged he wouldn't come back for ten years, by which time things might have settled down. Solon set off on a world tour. Among the places he visited was the city of Sais in Egypt. There some temple priests told him an astounding story.

Our planet, claimed the priests, had been visited in

ATLANTIS

prehistory by a series of cataclysms so devastating that they destroyed whole civilisations and came close to wiping out the entire human race. A shattered humanity, climbing back from the brink of destruction, was so focused on survival that the art of writing was lost. Without records, people stopped believing in the disasters after just a few generations. Stories handed down about them became distorted into myths. Only Egypt, protected by its location, kept written histories of what really happened.

The priests then led Solon to a massive pillar, heavily

Atlantis

LOST CIVILISATION

inscribed with hieroglyphs (Ancient Egyptian symbols). There they translated a history that showed how much the world owed to Solon's native Athens and the courage of that city's army.

It appeared from the inscription that years before, there had been a chain of islands stretching across the Atlantic Ocean, so close together that coastal sailors could hop from one to the other until they reached the distant Americas. The largest of these islands was a continent 'bigger than Libya and Asia (Minor) put together'. It was called Atlantis.

Chapter 9
CATACLYSM ATLANTIS

Atlantis developed an advanced, warlike civilisation that expanded to take over the entire chain of islands. This island empire then colonised parts of South America before moving eastwards to conquer parts of North Africa and Mediterranean Europe as far as Tyrrhenia, a country that now forms part of modern Italy.

Despite (or possibly because of) their astonishing military successes, the ten kings of Atlantis wanted to enlarge their massive empire even further. They had their eyes on the remaining countries of the Mediterranean, notably Egypt and the various city states of Greece.

A great navy of trireme warships, three banks of oarsmen on each side, was sent through the Straits of Gibraltar to reinforce the troops already stationed in North Africa on Egypt's borders. Atlantean armies in

Tyrrhenia – then a Greek province – were also put on high alert. War was inevitable and the countries of the Mediterranean seemed powerless before such a mighty invader.

When fighting did break out, the conflict at first went in favour of Atlantis. Country after country fell and was occupied. The city states of Greece rose up and toppled one by one. It looked as if the war was over. The last great power, Egypt, lay open and helpless. In Greece, only plucky little Athens remained to be subdued.

But then something happened that seemed little short of miraculous. Athens, isolated and alone, abandoned by all her allies, fought on so bravely – and so skilfully – that she actually defeated the invader. And not only did Athens send the Atlantean fleet scurrying back to its island kingdom, but pressed on to free every Atlantean colony on the shores of the Mediterranean.

ATLANTIS

Although defeated in this war, Atlantis continued to flourish. The island was entirely self sufficient in foodstuffs and raw materials. Fruit farming was widespread, as was the growth of cereal crops. The climate was so good that the Atlanteans managed two harvests a year with the help of irrigation. The wilder parts of the continent were lush enough to support a variety of wildlife, including herds of elephants – an animal that consumes some 200 kilograms of vegetation every day.

There were extensive forests – hence plentiful timber. The Atlanteans engaged in large-scale mining of various metals. Industries included shipbuilding – the country had a standing navy of 1,200 vessels, even in peacetime – and the production of fruit juices and vegetable oils.

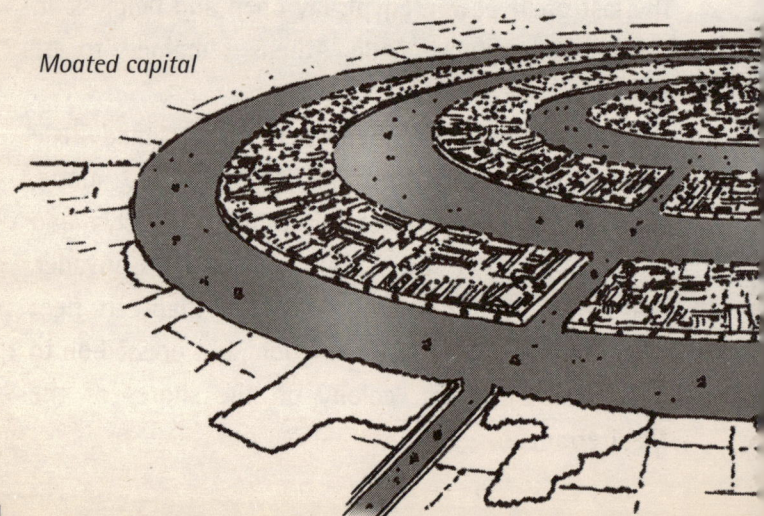

Moated capital

CATACLYSM ATLANTIS

Beaten back by the armies of Athens, the people of Atlantis returned to their familiar pursuits – the construction of temples, palaces, docks and bridges. Their moated capital, situated centrally on the island, was approached by a gigantic canal 90 metres wide, 30 metres deep and some 7,700 metres long.

Even this was not the most impressive of their engineering achievements. Solon's writings, penned around 570 BC, insist they built an artificial ditch around the country's entire central plain. It was 30 metres deep, about 180 metres wide and just short of an astonishing *two million* metres long.

If you put the various elements of Solon's description together, you get a picture of a civilisation capable of farming, food processing, mining and metal work. Its people knew how to read and write and were

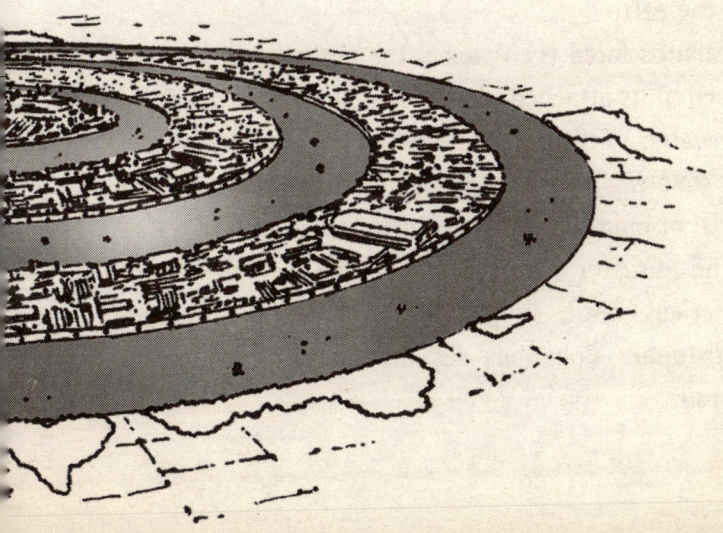

able to produce sophisticated artworks. They had domesticated the horse and learned how to make wine. They clothed themselves in colourful textiles. Their soldiers wore armour and carried metal weapons.

Descriptions of the Altantean navy suggest it could sail across oceans. Atlantis seems to have invented the chariot. Its engineering abilities could be set against those of the modern world.

Yet sometime after the war with Athens, Atlantis was destroyed in a cataclysm so violent that not a trace was left. According to Solon, it took no more than a single day and night to wipe out this mighty civilisation. Massive earthquakes and enormous floods struck large areas of our planet. Athens – the original Athens that had fought so bravely – was completely destroyed. Its buildings toppled, its people were scattered and its huge army was literally swallowed up by the earth.

Atlantis fared even worse. The entire continent and much of its attached island chain plunged beneath the icy waters of the ocean, almost killing every living soul. All that was left were floating debris and a massive shoal of mud that disrupted shipping for years.

The disaster effectively cut off access to the Americas until, long after they were forgotten, Christopher Columbus set off on his epic voyage in 1492.

Chapter 10

LAND OF GOLD

Solon wrote down the history of Atlantis, but never got around to making it public. The account might have been lost forever if it hadn't fallen into the hands of a relative named Critias. Critias preserved Solon's papers in the family archives and handed them down to his descendants. His grandson, also called Critias, told the story to a Greek philosopher named Plato.

Plato, who lived between 428 and 348 BC, remains to this day one of the most respected names of the ancient world. His works are studied by scholars, discussed in universities, translated and reprinted around the globe. He was so taken by what Critias told him that he included

Plato

an account in his own writings.

Plato's version of prehistory not only describes the vast cataclysm that sank Atlantis and destroyed the original civilisation of Ancient Greece, but also contains detailed information about Atlantean culture, including a bizarre custom observed by the ten kings who ruled the island continent.

Plato named nine of the kings as Ampheres, Autochthon, Azaes, Diaprepes, Elasippus, Evaemon, Gadeirus, Mestor and Mneseus. The tenth, Atlas, was described as their hereditary Emperor. They met together every fifth and sixth year, alternating because they wanted to honour both the odd and even number.

If Atlantis Existed, Where Are the Fossils?

Your textbooks talk about humanity's 'fossil record' as if it was a big deal. In fact, it's one of the most misleading, scrappy sources of information you could possibly consult. Here are some forbidden facts about fossils:

- 99.9% of all the organisms that ever lived have disappeared without leaving the slightest trace.

- Of the estimated 30 billion species produced by our world, only 250,000 have so far turned up in the fossil record.

> 🐚 95% of the fossil record is composed of sea creatures. The chances of fossilisation for anything living on land are very low indeed.
>
> 🐚 If the entire population of America was wiped out tomorrow, the fossil record would (statistically) contain no more than 50 bones – far less than a full skeleton – assuming anybody ever found them.

The place for their meeting was impressive. They gathered in a temple to Poseidon, a god associated with the sea and also with violent earthquakes.

The building was enormous. Its length is given as a *stadium* and it was exactly half as wide as it was long. Because the length of a stadium varied in the ancient world, you can't be sure of its exact size, but it was probably about 180 metres long and could have been as much as 215 metres. That makes it bigger than St Paul's Cathedral in London.

The temple architecture was fantastic and awe-inspiring. It featured a series of finely worked pinnacles, perhaps a little similar to the minarets of the Middle East. Every wall was covered in plate silver. The pinnacles were plated with gold.

Lavish use of precious materials didn't end there. Walk inside and your eyes would be drawn to an ivory

ATLANTIS

ceiling intricately worked with gold, silver and something called orichalcum.

In Roman times, the name orichalcum was given to an alloy of copper and zinc – a type of brass – but the word seems to refer to something else here. Brass was known all right, but 'orichalcum' was described as a warm, reddish metal dug directly from the earth, not an alloy of any sort. It was thought to be the most valuable of all metals except gold. Walls, floor and pillars of the temple were coated with it.

The use of gold itself was just as extravagant. Dominating the entire temple was a golden statue of the god so enormous that its head brushed the ceiling high above. Poseidon stood in a massive golden chariot drawn by six winged golden horses. As if this were not enough, the centrepiece was surrounded by *100* life-sized statues of nereids – mythic sea nymphs – riding on leaping dolphins ... all in solid gold.

Although everything else paled by comparison with this amazing display, wealthy citizens endowed many precious metal statues throughout the building. Set around the outside were statues of the kings themselves, each accompanied by his wife, each again made in solid gold. Even the enclosure wall was gold.

Chapter 11

ROYAL HUNT

The Temple of Poseidon took pride of place in the central, moated citadel that was the heart of the city. In many ways, its surroundings were as impressive as the temple itself.

There seems to be some suggestion that the kingdom had volcanic hot springs like those you find in Iceland today. But whether the source was natural or artificial, the kingdom's engineers created two massive fountains, one running with warm water, the other with cold. Around them they erected various ornamental buildings, including public bathhouses. These were interplanted with exotic trees. At one spot there was a particularly beautiful sacred grove, dedicated to Poseidon.

Lesser gods were not forgotten – there were many other temples, a few of which almost rivalled the main one in size. There were also gardens and gymnasiums

ROYAL HUNT

for the athletic men and women of the kingdom. Surrounding the area was an enormous stadium used for the country's favourite sport, horse racing. Throughout this setting roamed herds of wild bulls.

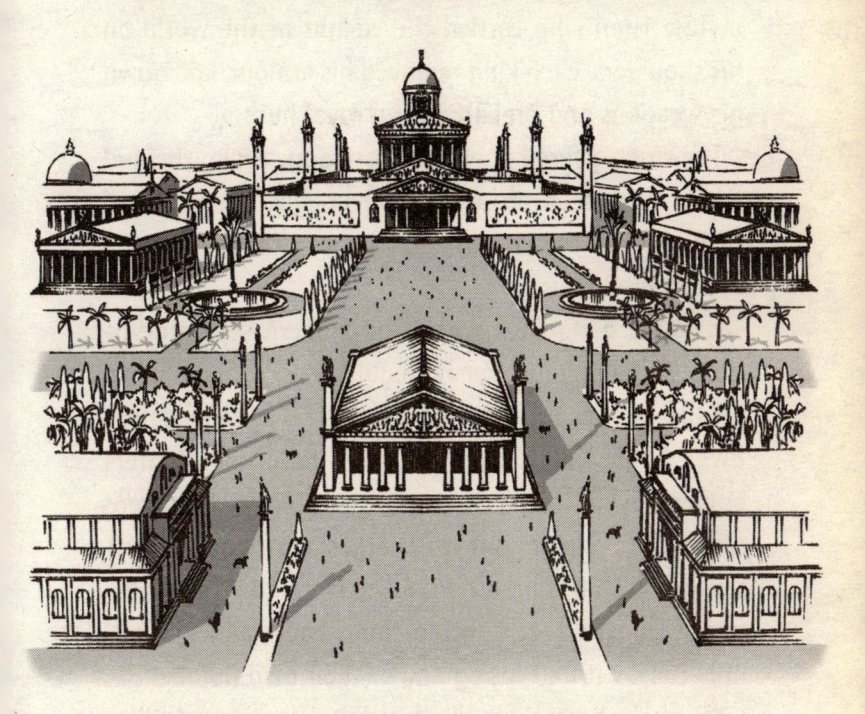

Bulls were respected elsewhere in the ancient world as symbols of virility and power. They were mummified in Egypt and took part in sacred games on the island of Crete. But here the ferocious creatures served an altogether more gruesome purpose.

When the kings met, they first discussed their differences and tried to pinpoint any of their number

ATLANTIS

who might have broken the ancient laws. Then they embarked on a bizarre ceremony.

Under the direction of Emperor Atlas, a man so powerful that his name was later attached to the mythic Titan who carried the weight of the world on his shoulders, each king removed his armour, laid down his weapons and prepared for a royal hunt.

The kings offered prayers to Poseidon, asking the god to lead them to an acceptable animal. Then, armed with no more than a stake and a noose, they moved off in search of their prey.

It was a dangerous game. The modern stampede of bulls in Pamplona, Spain, regularly kills and maims people, despite the fact that everyone is running to *get away* from the ferocious beasts. Here the hunters boldly moved towards them, for the ancient kings were pledged to single out the largest, strongest, most savage bull, cut him off from the remainder of the ill-tempered herd and bring him back alive – all, hopefully, without losing any of their own number.

When the animal was captured, it was dragged to an orichalcum pillar situated in the temple. The pillar featured two very different, interlinked inscriptions. One detailed the country's legal code. The other was a magical oath that called down mighty curses on the head of anyone who disobeyed the laws.

The bull was taken to the pillar and sacrificed by having its throat cut so that blood spattered on the sacred oath. The remainder of the bull's blood was carefully collected as the animal died, then the carcass was cut up and burned on a massive sacrificial fire. A large bowl was filled with wine and ten clots of bull's blood – one for each king – were added.

One after another, the kings stepped forward to fill a golden cup with the bloodwine. The first drink was poured directly on the sacrificial fire, as king after king swore to make his judgements in accordance with the laws written on the pillar and, further, to be bound personally by them.

This done, they drank the wine until darkness fell and the sacrificial fire died down. Then they put on ceremonial azure (blue) robes and sat throughout the night considering cases and handing down judgements. When day broke, they wrote down their decisions on a golden tablet which, with their robes, was dedicated and stored forever in the temple.

Chapter 12

WHERE WAS ATLANTIS?

Ask your teachers, or any other scholars, about the account of Atlantis given in the last two chapters and they'll tell you it's a story dreamed up by Plato to illustrate the possibility of an ideal state.

But Plato himself denied that. He presented Atlantis as fact, a fragment of hidden history. This was confirmed by one of his early followers, Crantor, who took the trouble of interviewing several Egyptian priests. They not only confirmed Solon's story, but showed him columns of hieroglyphs that gave the complete account.

This wasn't the only confirmation. The geographer Marcellus, who lived in the 1st century BC, recorded the existence of three large and seven small Atlantic islands inhabited by people who kept traditions of Atlantis and its empire. In more recent times, various explorers, romantics, cranks and even scientists have set out to locate Atlantis, with varying results.

Back in 1925, the famous explorer, Colonel P.H. Fawcett, got it into his head that Atlantis lay in the heart of the Brazilian jungle. He set off to find it and was never seen again. A diving expedition in 1953 found undersea rock walls at a depth of 14 metres near Heligoland and concluded that they were remnants of Atlantis. An archaeologist named Leo Frobenius decided the lost continent was actually Nigeria. Another, Adolf Schulten, placed it in southern Spain.

These theories didn't stop geographer Albert Hermann locating it in Tunisia. Others have placed it in Portugal, France, England, Sweden, Belgium, Prussia, Italy, Spitsbergen, Iran, Ceylon, the Caucuses Mountains, Russia's Azov Sea, and off the coast of Holland.

In 1968, marine archaeologists found a huge underwater wall in the Bahamas and started people claiming that it must be an Atlantis remnant. Eighteen years later, two Canadian authors were arguing that Atlantis was actually Antarctica.

This theory cut no ice with the Russian Academy of Sciences which sponsored a diving expedition in 1998 to a location 160 kilometres (100 miles) off the coast of Cornwall. At much the same time, the English explorer Colonel John Blashford-Snell set off to prove his own conviction that Atlantis had flourished in Bolivia, South America.

Few of these locations fit in with Plato's description of Atlantis and its island chain as lying just beyond the Straits of Gibraltar. But one respected scholar, the French prehistorian and geologist, Jacques Collina-Girard of the University of Provence, has gone on record with support for Plato's claims.

Professor Collina-Girard realised there was accepted geological evidence of a major rise in sea levels around the time Atlantis was supposed to have sunk. This led him to investigate what the geography of the area must have been like *before* sea levels rose.

What he discovered was startling. Underwater surveys showed that before the rise there really had been an island chain near the Straits of Gibraltar. What's more, the major island of the chain – while smaller than Plato described – was located more or less where Plato had placed Atlantis. Furthermore, all the evidence showed this island disappeared at exactly the time Plato specified.

Professor Collina-Girard's work would seem to establish some physical basis for the Atlantis story. But today's historians will not accept the idea of an island civilisation. Their basic problem is the timing. Since we know the year in which Solon visited Egypt and the time span mentioned by the priests, it's possible to calculate that the Empire of Atlantis arose many years before 9600 BC.

That would put it in the middle of the Ice Age, when our deep-freeze world was far too cold for civilisation to develop.

Chapter 13

ICE AGE THEORY

Scientists, and many of your teachers, have an unfortunate habit of presenting the Ice Age as if it was established fact. In reality, it's largely guesswork. Here's how it got into your textbooks.

The science of geology, which studies the physical make-up of our planet, is just over 200 years old. The earliest geologists were faced with a mystery. As they looked around their world, it became obvious something very dramatic had happened in relatively recent times.

The evidence was all around them. Country after country was strewn with debris. Millions of boulders had been carried from their original homes and deposited hundreds, sometimes thousands of kilometres away. Boulders from Scandinavia were scattered across Germany. Huge stones from Finland ended up in Poland. They perched delicately on

ICE AGE THEORY

mountain peaks, choked whole valleys or stood in splendid isolation in meadows.

Some of the stones were enormous. One in Sweden was 5 kilometres (3 miles) long. An entire English village was built on another that bedded down on the east coast. There was a little one in Ohio that weighed 13,500 tonnes. The question was: what moved them?

In the late 1700s, everybody knew the answer. These stones, which were known as *erratics*, had been washed across the globe by the Flood – the same Flood described in the Bible when it rained for forty days and nights and God told Noah to build an ark.

In 1802, only John Playfair disagreed. He was a British mathematician who decided it wasn't water that carried the erratics, but

Erratic

rivers of ice – huge glaciers. He published his theory and everybody ignored it.

But in 1837, Louis Agassiz marched onto the scene. Agassiz studied fossil fish and was blessed with a fertile imagination. In an address to a learned society in

Switzerland, he vividly described a chilling world of ice stretching from the North Pole to the Mediterranean. The proof, he said, lay not just in the erratics but in the polished surfaces of some rocks and the lines or ridges seen on many others. These effects were the result of glaciers scraping the stone.

Agassiz was a persuasive speaker, but not persuasive enough. One member of his audience told him to go back to his fossil fish. Undiscouraged, Agassiz spent the next ten years travelling to seek support for his theory. A breakthrough came when it was taken up by the British geologist Sir Charles Lyell. Lyell was the big scientific cheese of his day. His books were the standard textbooks of geology. His ideas were (and still are) widely accepted. His reputation was enormous. He firmly believed all geological change was gradual and liked the idea that erratics had been moved by the slow creep of ice.

With Lyell backing him, there was no holding Agassiz. He suggested temperatures had plunged repeatedly in prehistoric times and a sea of ice had covered almost all of northern and western Europe, extending down across the western reaches of the Mediterranean into North Africa as far as the Atlas Mountains. He believed immense ice sheets had covered north west Asia and much of North America. Only the topmost peaks of mountain ranges emerged from these vast frozen wastes like solitary islands.

ICE AGE THEORY

World temperatures dropped like a stone. Close to the ice sheets they dropped to minus 6°C or below. Over an area of permafrost stretching hundreds of kilometres, they never climbed above zero. Beyond this the air temperature was anything up to 20°C lower than it is today.

Urged on by Lyell, scientists got so used to the idea of an Ice Age that they came to accept it as an established fact. Once that happened, Ice Ages started to pop up again and again in the scientific picture of prehistory. A Scots geologist named Andrew Ramsay announced evidence of not one, but two. Others increased the figure to 'three or four' then 'five or six' then 'seven or more'. Soon scientists came to believe that the last two and a half million years had been one mega Ice Age broken up by brief periods of warmer weather.

Today Ice Age theory pushes back much further. Scientists think they've found evidence of extensive ice in such distant eras as the Cretaceous (144 million to 66.4 million years ago), the Permian (286 to 245 million), the Silurian (438 to 408 million) and the Precambrian (3.8 billion to 540 million years ago).

They talk confidently about 'glacial' erratics and 'ice scour' as if such things have now been proven beyond all possibility of doubt. But they haven't.

Chapter 14

CAUSES OF THE ICE AGE

Ice sheets can't move of their own accord. To cover the area Agassiz described, they had to be gravity driven. In other words, they had to come down from higher ground.

But that was all right. When Ice Age theory was originally put forward, several scientists suggested a massive range of extraordinarily high mountains must have risen at the North Pole during prehistoric times. Their rise pushed Arctic ice downwards and outwards to cover vast areas of the planet. The Ice Age ended when the polar mountains disappeared. Without fresh supplies, Agassiz's sea of ice just melted.

Disappearing mountains might sound a bit farfetched, but the great thing about the idea was that nobody could disprove it – at the time, explorers hadn't yet reached the North Pole. All the same, doubts crept in once geologists began to claim there'd been

CAUSES OF THE ICE AGE

not one but several Ice Ages. Did that mean polar mountains kept popping up and down like yo-yos?

When the first expedition finally reached the North Pole in 1909, nobody asked the explorers to look out for any remains of the famous Arctic mountains. Which was just as well, since nobody then or since has ever found the slightest trace of them.

But if it wasn't mountains, what caused the various Ice Ages? There's no lack of theories:

- *It was sun spots.* A massive increase in sun spots might cut down on the Sun's overall radiation, thus cooling down the Earth.

- *It was space clouds.* Some astronomers believe that every couple of million years or so our whole solar system drifts into a space cloud – an area filled with billions of tiny matter particles. These particles might well absorb enough sunshine to cool down the Earth.

- *It was volcanoes.* If enough of them erupted all at once, the amount of debris thrown into the atmosphere could block out the Sun and cool down the Earth.

▲ *It was a change in our planet's orbit.* If the orbit lengthened for some reason, that would cool down the Earth.

▲ *It was the movement of the Poles.* Scientists have discovered that both the North and South Poles of our planet have shifted measurably over the centuries. In certain circumstances this shift could cool down the Earth.

▲ *It was a reverse greenhouse effect.* Today we worry about the world heating up because of too much carbon dioxide in the atmosphere. A reverse of this – too little of the gas – would cool down the Earth.

▲ *It was a thickening of the ozone layer ... It was the upward movement of land masses ... It was a drastic change in climate ... It was continental drift ... It was a tilting of the Earth's axis ...* All or any of these things might well cool down the Earth.

It all sounds very convincing until you realise that cooling down the Earth won't cause an Ice Age. You need to heat it up for that. Here's how to start your own Ice Age ...

CAUSES OF THE ICE AGE

How to Start an Ice Age

✓ *Put a bowl of water in your freezer and it will turn into a bowl of ice. Put in an empty bowl and the only thing it will turn into is an empty frozen bowl. Cold on its own will never give you ice. There are no ice sheets covering Siberia, which is the coldest place on the planet. Before you can have ice, you need water.*

✓ *On Planet Earth, water comes from the oceans. The Sun's heat causes some of their water to evaporate. The evaporation forms clouds. Clouds produce rain. Rain creates lakes and rivers. Glaciers are frozen rivers.*

✓ *If you want to create an Ice Age like the one scientists believe gripped our world 10,000 years ago, you need to take so much water from the oceans that their level would drop by up to 300 metres.*

✓ *And you'd have to take the water out first.*

✓ *To do that, you'd have to heat up the world dramatically so vast quantities of water evaporated. Then you'd have to freeze that water almost instantly. (Cool it down slowly and it just finds its way back into the oceans.)*

A heat-up/flash-freeze cycle is the *only* way an Ice Age could be triggered. There's nothing in the whole of Ice Age theory to explain how such a weird cycle might come about. Apart from the difficulties of getting it started, there are many other problems with the theory of the Ice Age.

Chapter 15

FORBIDDEN FACTS ABOUT THE ICE AGE

Remember where Ice Age theory came from in the first place? Geologists kept finding erratics – huge stones that had been moved hundreds, sometimes thousands of kilometres across the globe. They eventually decided that the only thing that could have moved the stones was ice. But there are erratics in Mongolia, Uruguay and the Sahara Desert – all places everybody agrees were never glaciated.

The great ice sheets were supposed to have started in the far north and moved south. Yet they somehow managed to miss Aberdeenshire (in the far north of Scotland) altogether. Scientists claim evidence of ice in southern Scotland ... but not nearly enough ice to fit with Ice Age theory. Although ice sheets were supposed to have covered almost the whole of the

British Isles, there are large areas of England, Ireland, Scotland and Wales that show no signs of glaciation whatsoever.

There were supposed to have been ice sheets covering Alaska, several Arctic islands and, as we noted earlier, parts of Siberia. Millions of tonnes of moving ice would flatten anything in their path, yet in all these areas you'll find deep frozen trees and plants – not to mention slim spires of rock – that miraculously survived. You'll find rock spires off the Norwegian coast as well, despite the fact that they should have been flattened by the Scandinavian ice sheet as it expanded towards Britain.

The Scandinavian ice sheet is a bit of a bother really. If it carried the erratics that were deposited on the Dogger Bank, they should have arrived from the east. But all the signs are that they actually came from the north west. 'Ice scour' in the Outer Hebrides doesn't show an east-west movement either.

These aren't just local problems. If you examine hills and mountains for ice scour patterns, particularly in North America, you'll find them on the northern sides all right, but not the southern. That leaves you with a real mystery. The ice sheets moved down from the north, crept up the northern side of a mountain or hill, but apparently never came down the other side. Which is, of course, impossible.

It's also impossible for an ice sheet to move more

than 11 kilometres (7 miles) on a flat surface. If you try to push it further, the amount of force you exert will crush the ice. Agassiz didn't know that when he described his sea of ice creeping over several hundred kilometres of European plains. But the fact remains that the proposed movement of ice in the Ice Age contradicts the laws of physics.

Although nobody has ever found written texts dating from the Ice Age, the people who lived then have left us pictures of what life was like. So far we've found more than 270 sites in Europe that feature elaborate paintings on the walls of caves. You might wonder how people fighting tooth and nail for survival in a frozen world ever found time for art, but leave that to one side.

The paintings themselves depict scenes of hunting and battle, weapons, animals and sexual activity – in other words the things that were most important to the artists.

Yet nowhere is there a single representation of the ice sheets which, at their edges, were supposed to rise in glistening cliffs miles high. Even stranger, the people in the paintings are not shown dressed in furs like the familiar Inuit. Almost without exception, they are lightly clad or even naked. One archaeologist, Mary Settegast, wrote: "Fringed waistbands are common; animal skins are occasionally shown around the waist with tails hanging down; and while some of the warriors appear to be wearing 'knee-breeches' or loincloths, others wear nothing at all." How long could you survive in an Ice Age wearing just a loincloth or nothing at all?

It's possible, I suppose, that Ice Age artists *just imagined* those around them were stark naked, but there have been finds that contradict this notion. Fossil footprints of children and adults in caves at Fontanet, Aldene, and Tuc d'Audoubert in France and several other sites all show the people of the Ice Age went round barefoot.

Chapter 16

BIG MISTAKES

Can scientists get such important things so badly wrong? Of course they can – they've been getting things badly wrong for years. Fossils of extinct animals began to turn up in the early 19th Century. Experts promptly put them together and published pictures of the result – weird monsters that look nothing like the dinosaurs you see illustrated in the textbooks today. Next time you're in London, pay a visit to Crystal Palace Park in Sydenham. There you can see the world's first life size concrete model of an *iguanodon*. Its thumb is sticking out of its nose and it stands on four legs instead of two.

In 1912, an amateur British archaeologist named

BIG MISTAKES

Charles Dawson discovered parts of a skull, a jawbone and some teeth in a Sussex gravel pit. Experts gave an age of 500,000 years to the fragments and interpreted them as the missing link between humanity and apes. Nearby finds over the next two years confirmed these first discoveries and showed the primitive Briton had used a hand axe to carve himself a cricket bat out of an elephant's thighbone.

The cricket bat might sound like something from *The Flintstones*, but archaeologists took it – and the other items – very seriously. At one time they even argued that the finds proved we couldn't be descended from the *Australopithecines*.

But then in 1953 – that's more than *forty years* after the original discovery – a South African professor named Joe Weiner finally exposed the whole thing as a fake.

The bones weren't anything like 500,000 years old: they'd just been stained and painted to look that way. Some of the teeth had been filed, some of the bones whittled into shape with a knife. The flint tools had been manufactured in the 20th Century, as had that ridiculous 'cricket bat.' The jawbone wasn't even human: it belonged to a female orang-utan.

Scientists can make mistakes all right. The trick is to figure out exactly when they're making them. To do that, you have to think for yourself, take nothing on trust and, above all, don't automatically believe

ATLANTIS

something just because the person telling you is called a scientist. Because usually what you're dealing with isn't evidence – it's the *interpretation* of evidence. For more than a century now, science has built up a picture of the way early humanity lived based on the discovery of ancient tools – pieces of flint carefully knapped to produce primitive blades, arrowheads and axes. Those pieces of flint are the evidence and nobody doubts their reality. To call them ancient tools is an *interpretation* of the evidence. You might ask yourself is that interpretation correct?

A few years before he started digging in the Sussex gravel pit, Charles Dawson turned up at a meeting of his local antiquarian society dragging a sackful of flint. He walked to the front of the meeting, dumped his sack on the floor then, to the absolute astonishment of his colleagues, began to jump up and down on it. When the uproar died down, he tipped the shattered flint out of the sack. Many of the fragments were absolutely identical to the so-called stone tools of ancient man.

Did Dawson's demonstration persuade his fellow scientists they might be wrong about the sort of things people used back in the Stone Age? Did it heck as like! They just stopped speaking to him. But if scientists (at least some scientists) won't question their own conclusions, it's up to us to do it for them. Given the evidence presented in the last few chapters, you might think their theory of an Ice Age is long overdue for questioning.

Chapter 17
IMPOSSIBLE ATLANTIS

Even if you leave aside the thorny question of the Ice Age, prehistorians still insist Atlantis is impossible.

Plato described a prehistoric civilisation more than 11,500 years old that:

- Developed writing.
- Created artworks.
- Domesticated the horse.
- Mined copper.
- Worked metal.
- Fermented wine.
- Built ocean-going ships.
- Used pottery.
- Grew crops.

IMPOSSIBLE ATLANTIS

- **Knew about irrigation.**
- **Wove fabrics and tailored clothes.**
- **Moved huge quantities of stone.**
- **Embarked on major engineering works.**
- **Went to war.**

Spend a little time in your nearest reference library and you'll soon see why your teachers and most scientists consider Atlantis is pure fiction. They'll claim just about everything mentioned has been well researched and documented. In each and every case, the textbooks will tell you these developments came far later – by many thousands of years – than the 9600 BC date assigned by Plato to Atlantis.

Here's what you'll be told:

1. Writing was invented by the Sumerians sometime during the third millennium BC

2. Art is a sign of civilisation. You may find a few crude paintings and roughly carved figurines before the cities arose in Mesopotamia, but nothing worth writing home about.

3. Horses were first domesticated for their meat and skins, later as a means of transport. Nobody knows exactly when it happened, but probably not less than 1,000 years after Atlantis is supposed to have

ATLANTIS

sunk. For the sort of big stadium horse races Plato described you'd have to wait even longer. Such races simply couldn't have taken place in a stone stadium before the Sumerians started building cities in 3300 BC and to be honest, there's not much evidence of them until a lot later.

4   There is evidence of the world's first copper mining in southeast Europe somewhere between 4000 and 4500 BC – far too late for Atlantis.

5   People only started working metal the way Plato described around 3200 BC

6   There's no doubt the Egyptians were drinking wine in 2500 BC but to suggest people were making wine thousands of years earlier is like suggesting they were all driving around in Ferraris.

7   The earliest you'll find evidence for boats of any sort is the fourth millennium BC and you'll find it in Egypt. Some of them were huge because they were designed to carry massive stones, but none of them ventured beyond the Nile. That didn't happen for nearly 1000 years when the Egyptians began to sail the Mediterranean and Red Seas. It was a further 2,000 years before anybody was sailing the great oceans.

8   Excavations at a Stone Age settlement in Turkey unearthed the world's first pottery, dating to

about 7000 BC It was fairly crude stuff, sun-dried rather than fired. Since it took another 500 years to produce anything remotely like the pottery we use today, you can see why prehistorians can't swallow the idea of real pottery in Atlantis.

9 Farming didn't start until the end of the Ice Age. Everybody knows that.

10 Canals and irrigation systems like those described by Plato were certainly known in the ancient world. Nineveh, the oldest city of the Assyrian Empire (situated opposite modern Mosul in Iraq), had a stone-lined canal to bring it water, for example ... although this wasn't built until the 7th Century BC

11 The idea that Atlanteans wore proper clothes is another nonsense. At the time Atlantis was supposed to have flourished, northern Europeans were making garments of animal skins sewn together with leather thongs. Weaving didn't come into its own until the rise of the Middle Eastern civilisations.

12 The earliest people to move really large stones were the Ancient Egyptians, who transported them up to 500 miles to build their Great Pyramid. But that didn't happen until 2600 BC at the earliest.

13 The Great Pyramid wasn't the earliest example of

ATLANTIS

major engineering works in the ancient world. There were several very impressive structures created earlier... but only a few hundred years earlier, not 7,000.

14 It's possible to date the time when humanity first invented war. Just look for the earliest walled cities. (You can keep out wild animals with a simple fence – it takes a stone wall to keep out an attacking army.) Since there were no walled cities before the fourth millennium BC, you can safely say there was no war either.

So there you have it. The details of Plato's account positively prove an ancient civilisation like Atlantis could never have existed. Assuming you believe what your teachers tell you...

Chapter 18

FORBIDDEN FACTS ABOUT EARLY WRITING

Some years ago, a very curious piece of reindeer antler was discovered in a cave near Lussac-les-Chateaux in Western France. It was estimated by archaeologists to be more than 14,000 years old and engraved with a picture of a tubby horse. It seemed at first glance to be just one more example of those crude animal artworks carved by our distant ancestors in the cold prehistory of the Stone Age.

But closer examination disclosed a whole series of little marks, carefully arranged in rows, blocks, curving and dead straight lines. Under expert analysis, these turned out not to be just random decoration but 'an artificial memory system which could record different categories of information.'

This cautious analysis appears to have been carefully worded in order to avoid a startling conclusion – the nomadic hunters of deep prehistory were able to read and write. For what, after all, is a memory system that records information if not a form of writing?

The reindeer bone is not the only example of writing that clearly predates the earliest Sumerian script. The distinguished archaeologist Marija Gumbutas noted that a wide variety of Stone Age symbols – crosses, spirals, arrangements of dots and so on – appeared on pots, lamps and figurines of the period. After 20 years of study, she came to the conclusion they represented a sophisticated alphabet that expressed the religious world-view of the time. The cross, for example, represented the four corners of the Earth and symbolised the cycle of the year, renewal, and the Great Goddess universally worshipped in prehistoric Europe. The spiral represented life itself and the powers of nature.

In 1979, two American academics, Allan Forbes Jr.

and T. R. Crowder, took it on themselves to carry out an analysis of some curious signs that appear repeatedly in Stone Age cave art. Cave paintings that include these signs are at least 25,000 years old – dating to an era long before Atlantis sank – and are found not just in Europe but right across the world as far as distant China.

If you look at the examples of these signs below, you'll probably agree they look nothing like the bulk of the cave paintings you see reproduced in the history books. They don't look like animals. They don't look like people. They don't look like weapons or tools or pottery bowls. In fact they don't look like anything very much.

↑ 🏠 🛏 ‖ ☉ ⫼ H

So what are they? Forbes and Crowder first saw the signs as property marks, a little like the cattle brands of the Wild West. But it made no sense to paint a number of different marks on your property when one would do just as well. And if each mark represented a different owner, how come whole rows of them appear on the same piece of (cave) property?

Next they considered the possibility that the signs were hunting tallies – a record of the number of

ATLANTIS

reindeer or aurochs slaughtered for food. That didn't work out too well either. After all, if you want to count something, it's a lot easier to carve a few notches on a piece of wood. Were the signs perhaps memory aids? Maybe ... but if you'd a good enough memory to recall a great number of these signs (those shown on the previous page are only a tiny fragment of the total) then you hardly need aids.

The breakthrough came when the two Americans compared the prehistoric symbols with characters found in early writing like Greek and Runic. The conclusion was inescapable. 'The sole remaining possibility is writing ... not differing fundamentally from inscriptions in early written languages,' they themselves wrote in a paper on the subject. On the basis of this evidence it would seem Plato's claim that writing was invented before 9600 BC now stands up to scientific scrutiny.

ᚠᚾᛏᚲᛉᛒᚦᛁᛗᚠᛪᛗᚱᛋ

But Forbes and Crowder also wrote: 'The proposition that Ice Age reindeer hunters invented writing 15,000 years ago or more is utterly unthinkable... If [they] invented writing thousands of years before civilisation arose in the Near East, then our most cherished beliefs about the nature of society and the course of human development would be demolished.'

Which may explain why you still won't find any mention of Stone Age writing in your school books.

Chapter 19

FORBIDDEN FACTS ABOUT PREHISTORIC ART

The development of art is something that happened long before the textbooks date the first civilisations. In 1833, Dr François Mayor of Geneva discovered the first ever artwork dating to the Old Stone Age. While exploring a cave near the French-Swiss border, he came across what he took to be an ancient harpoon made from antler. But closer examination showed something had been done to this 'harpoon' that would have rendered it virtually useless for spearing fish. It had been delicately and expertly carved to resemble a budding plant. Dr Mayor rooted around some more and unearthed another piece of antler decorated with an engraving of a bird.

Thirty-one years later an even more intriguing antler

turned up in the same cave. It was engraved with a plant on one side and an ibex on the other.

These were just the first of many similar finds including a horse-head engraved in antler, a reindeer foot bone decorated with representations of two hinds and a long-extinct mammoth engraved on a fragment of its own ivory. It transpired that similar engravings had been discovered earlier, but thrown away or ignored because they were so well done that everybody thought they were modern carvings.

Examples of ancient carvings were exhibited at the Paris Universal Exhibition of 1878. One visitor who saw them was a Spanish landowner named Don Marcelino Sanz de Sautuola, who was so intrigued that he was determined to hunt for such artefacts himself.

One of the sites he examined was a cave at Altamira, near the northern coast of Spain, which had been discovered when a local hunter freed his dog from some rocks. Don de Sautuola began to excavate the cave in 1879 and in November of that year was digging in the cave floor when his little daughter Maria suddenly called out, "Look, Papa – oxen!" Don de Sautuola followed her pointing finger and, to his astonishment, saw there was a colourful cluster of bison painted on the ceiling. It was the first of many marvellous artworks that decorated the cave.

When word of the discovery got out, visitors flocked to Altamira, including the Spanish King Alfonso XII, who committed a royal act of vandalism by writing his name in candle-black near the entrance. One of Spain's greatest palaeontologists (fossil experts), Professor Juan Vilanova y Piera, visited the cave and pronounced the artworks genuine. But despite his support, the academic establishment rejected the pictures *en masse*. The most influential prehistorian in France, Emile Cartailhac, referred to the art as 'a dauber's vulgar joke' and told Don de Sautuola that the 'wild cattle' in the paintings looked nothing like the real prehistoric animals and had differently shaped horns.

Expert after expert condemned the paintings ... usually after refusing to look at them. One who did turn up was Edouard Harlé, and he reported in the most influential prehistory journal of the day that they dated no earlier than the 1870s. They were, he said, too good to have been done by 'prehistoric savages,' anatomically inaccurate, and applied with a modern paintbrush. He claimed the paint was so fresh it came away on his finger.

Others went even further, accusing de Sautuola himself of having forged the paintings, or at least commissioned a modern expert to do the job for him.

ATLANTIS

The Don took the accusations as an attack on his honour and fell into a decline from which he died prematurely in 1888. Despite the tragic outcome, it remains possible to understand the logic of the experts' position. The art was so sophisticated in its execution, so technically advanced in style, that it was impossible to believe it could have been created by primitive hunters battling the hostile environment of an Ice Age.

But created it was. More cave paintings were subsequently discovered in France and it quickly became obvious Don de Sautuola could not have run around forging them all. Today, nearly 300 decorated sites have been found in Europe alone. One painting of a galloping horse showed its legs in a position that cannot be seen by the naked eye, but was confirmed by high-speed photography in the 20th Century.

There have been subsequent discoveries of artworks, many incredibly beautiful and showing a high degree of technical sophistication, in Arabia, Australia, Brazil, China, India, Japan, Korea, Kwazulu in South Africa, Mexico, Namibia, North America, Patagonia, Peru, Portugal, Sicily, Zaire and Zimbabwe.

Some are as old as 30,000 years and may be 10,000 years older. All of them support Plato's claim that artistic creativity was well in place at the time of Atlantis.

Chapter 20

A MUSEUM OF FORBIDDEN FACTS

So far we've dealt with only two forbidden facts that have a bearing on the Atlantis story – the existence of prehistoric writing and prehistoric art. But if you take the trouble to do the research, you'll find a whole museum of forbidden facts, every one of which provides evidence supporting the tale Plato told.

Horses

Plato claimed the Atlanteans raced horses. The experts say the horse was not domesticated – anywhere on Earth – for several thousand years after Atlantis is supposed to have disappeared. But examine the sketch overleaf, faithfully copied from a drawing on a cave wall at La Marche in France. You'll note the horse is wearing a bridle, clear evidence that you're looking at a picture of a domesticated animal. Is that really a bridle? Perhaps there are cracks or marks on the cave wall that just happen to look like a bridle. Are you safe to draw conclusions from a single drawing?

Perhaps not, but there are at least two other engravings of bridled horses, one found at the Grotte de Marsoulas and the other in St Michel d'Arudy. Like the one at La Marche, they are more than 17,000 years old.

Mining

Plato claimed the Atlanteans mined copper and worked metal. The experts say this is nonsense. Yet people were actually mining copper before they got around to mining flint in Serbia. Furthermore, there are prehistoric copper mines, dated to periods long before Atlantis sank, on Lake Superior, in California, Arkansas, New Mexico, Missouri, Illinois, Indiana, Georgia and New Jersey.

In Ohio, there is evidence not only of copper mining, but also the prehistoric smelting of iron, indicating that the ancient peoples were metal workers. In Zambia they mined manganese (used in making copper, aluminium and steel) 28,130 years ago – confirmed by carbon dating of the site.

Wine

Plato claimed the Atlanteans drank wine. In 1980, two intact bottles of wine were excavated from a Chinese tomb dating to 1300 BC. Sites in the Eastern European country of Georgia have produced seeds of cultivated grapes and wine storage jars dating to 5000 BC. Both sets of finds are, of course, too recent to have direct bearing on the Atlantis situation, but by a curious quirk of nature, we can be confident that neither bottles nor jars are necessary to prove the existence of wine.

Next time you're presented with a bunch of grapes, take a moment to examine one before you savage them. You'll notice that the skin has a powdery coating. This is called the bloom and consists of pure yeast. Wine is created by the action of yeast on the sugar present in grape juice. (The yeast eats the sugar and excretes alcohol, gross though it sounds.) So to create wine, all you need do is crush some grapes and leave the pulp in the warm for a few days. It won't be great wine and it won't be strong wine, but it will be wine with an alcohol content.

This natural reaction makes grapes and wine inseparable. Where you find one, you will inevitably

ATLANTIS

find the other. Exactly the same process happens with the marula fruit in Africa. When it falls from the tree, natural yeasts quickly transform it into an alcoholic pulp. Elephants are well aware of this process and during the season eat vast quantities of marula windfalls, then stagger away to sleep it off exactly like city drunks on a Saturday night.

Our distant ancestors were no less observant than elephants, so you can safely assume that where they ate grapes they drank wine. And seeds found in Turkey, Syria, Jordan and the Lebanon show they were eating grapes more than 10,000 years ago – around the time Atlantis sank.

Pottery

Plato claimed the Atlanteans knew about the potter's art, which contradicts the widespread academic belief that pottery was invented in the Near or Middle East. Although the textbooks talk about the Turkish finds of 7000 BC, there was pottery found in Iran that was 11,000 years old – within just 500 years of Plato's dating of Atlantis. But that's not the earliest pottery by a long chalk. In the 1960s, archaeologists investigating the Ishigoya Cave on the Japanese island of Honshu discovered a pottery jar dating to 10000 BC. Elsewhere on the island they found examples that were even older – dating back to a staggering 11000 BC. They weren't crude examples either. Even after 13,000 years you can still see the raised ropework beading around the rim and the remnants of complex decoration on the remainder of the pot.

Farming

Plato claimed the Atlanteans grew crops at a time when the Ice Age was supposedly in full swing. If you refuse to believe this, then you should logically refuse to believe that the Natufian tribes, living in Palestine around 9000 BC, were busily harvesting grain around the time Atlantis sank (and long before the supposed Ice Age ended) despite the fact that archaeologists have now found the sickles they used.

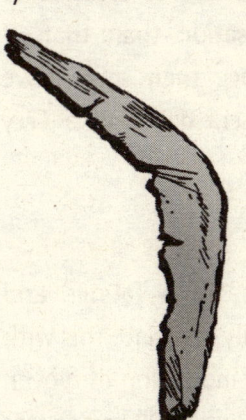

While you're at it, you might as well deny that people living in Spirit Cave, Thailand, grew domesticated beans, peas, gourds and water chestnuts around the same time ... something else firmly established by archaeological finds.

Irrigation

Plato claimed the Atlanteans built irrigation systems. Whatever your textbooks say, you don't have to wait until the time of King Sennacherib for evidence that this was entirely possible. In 1932, the explorer Captain G. E. H. Wilson reported on the prehistoric remains of irrigation systems – not to mention full-scale canals – in East Africa's Rift Valley.

There's also been the discovery in South America of a terrace-based irrigation system so technically advanced that, when restored, it proved capable of growing crops where modern farming methods had utterly failed. The terracing was at first credited to the Incas, a much later civilisation than that of Plato's fabled Atlantis, but since then there have been suggestions that the system dated to a very much earlier era.

Weaving

Plato claimed the Atlanteans wove fabrics and tailored clothes. Textbooks usually associate this with early civilisations. There is some indication of woven garments in southern Europe about 1,000 years after Atlantis was supposed to have sunk. But that's not where it stops. Excavation of ancient Russian burial sites in 1964 indicated people were tailoring their clothes as long ago as 20000 BC. Incredibly, they wore hats, shirts, trousers and moccasins.

Even more incredibly, a prehistoric mound at the famous archaeological site of Çatal Hüyük in Turkey has revealed fragments of woven linen, which seem at one time to have formed part of a woman's skirt.

War

Plato claimed the Atlanteans were a warlike people, long before historians believe humanity invented war. Can we be sure the historians are right? Most rock paintings and cave art depict animals rather than people, but in the Spanish Levant there are some striking exceptions to this rule. Here, overlooking the Mediterranean, you can see scene after scene of stick-like armies – mostly bowmen – locked in a most vicious battle. Coincidentally (or perhaps not) these unique artworks have been dated to the time Plato claimed Atlantis launched its great Mediterranean invasion.

Of course artists, even prehistoric artists, are supposed to use their imagination, but there is harder evidence. Excavations show a new type of arrowhead that suddenly appeared in huge quantities along the west European and Near Eastern coastlines at the time of the supposed invasion. If they didn't come from Atlantis, nobody has yet found out where they *did* come from.

Perhaps more to the point, burial sites in the region show signs of warrior deaths for the first time in the

ATLANTIS

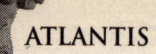

history of humanity. More than 100 graves have now been excavated that show skeletons with the new arrowheads lodged in their rib cages and spines.

This entire museum of forbidden facts supports point after point of Plato's story about lost Atlantis, showing that many things he claimed *could* actually have happened. All the same, an eagle-eyed reader like yourself will have noticed I skipped over three major aspects of the Atlantis story – the idea that its people were capable of moving large quantities of stone, building massive engineering works and navigating the deep oceans of the world.

But I only left those out because they all need chapters of their own.

Chapter 21

STONE MOVERS OF THE ANCIENT WORLD

There's a widespread idea that we do things better nowadays than at any other time in human history. When it comes to moving stone, that idea is just plain nonsense. Take the Great Pyramid of Egypt.

There are 2,300,000 blocks of stone in that old monster. Put together, they weigh 5,750,000 tonnes. Apart from the pyramid itself, there is a whole complex of associated stone-built structures – two temples, four lesser pyramids, several rectangular tombs (called mastabas) six boat pits and an elevated causeway. Most of the stone for this project was quarried locally. But some was dragged from Aswan, 800 kilometres (500 miles) to the south.

According to the experts, the Great Pyramid was built by a pharaoh named Khufu to serve as his tomb.

Khufu reigned from 2551 to 2528 BC, a period of 23 years. The combined mass of the pyramid complex has been estimated at 2,700,312 cubic metres. To build it within Khufu's lifetime, you'd have to shift 321.6 cubic metres of stone 24 hours a day, every day, for 8,395 days. In other words, you'd have to quarry, prepare, transport and lay a pyramid block (without time off for accidents, interruptions, deaths, disasters or total exhaustion) *every two minutes* day and night for 23 years.

We couldn't do that nowadays. The Indiana Limestone Institute of America was asked a few years ago how long it would take to quarry and ship enough limestone to duplicate the Great Pyramid. They estimated that using the most modern technology, including high explosives, power tools and diesel transport, the entire limestone industry of Indiana would need 81 years. That's just shifting the stone. You still have to build the pyramid.

Interestingly, nobody quite knows how the Ancient Egyptians actually did move those stones. Several years ago, Egyptologists discovered a picture that showed a giant statue of the Pharaoh being dragged along by teams of workmen using ropes. This is the only such picture ever discovered, but it was enough to get the BSM (Big Sweaty Men) Theory into the textbooks.

If you turn to any respectable academic source, you'll be told confidently that the Egyptians transported blocks of stone by tying ropes around them and harnessing them to teams of big sweaty men. Some sources will suggest they used sleds, pouring water ahead of them to ease the passage. Others imagine wooden rollers may have been the answer.

The trouble with the textbook method is that it doesn't work. In recent years, several archaeological teams have tried to move large blocks of stone in this way ... and failed miserably. The stones, often far smaller than those the Egyptians shifted, moved all right, but only over short distances and painfully slowly. Ropes broke, rollers shattered, sleds wore out and workmen were injured. Working at this rate, the Egyptians would still be trying to finish off their pyramids today.

ATLANTIS

Even what appears to be the relatively simple job of transporting local stone to the Great Pyramid remains something of a mystery. The sandstone and limestone that made up most of the vast structure was quarried just across the Nile. Egyptologists have always assumed, reasonably enough, that the blocks were hauled onto rafts and floated over the river. A Japanese television team decided to put this theory to the test. They built a sturdy wooden raft, hauled a single stone block onto it and pushed it out into the water. The raft sank.

The Egyptians weren't the only ancient culture to show that they could move stone far more efficiently than we can. There's a ruined city called Tiahuanaco near the southern shore of Lake Titicaca, in Bolivia. It has a Sun Temple as large as Trafalgar Square, in London. The entire city was constructed from stone blocks weighing up to 65 tonnes each. They bear no chisel marks, so how they were shaped remains a mystery, yet they fit together like pieces of an interlocking jigsaw.

The stone came from two different quarries. One supplied sandstone and was situated 16 kilometres (10 miles away). It shows signs of having produced blocks weighing up to 400 tonnes. The other supplied andesite from the slopes of an extinct volcano and was located 80.5 kilometres (50 miles away).

Tiahuanaco is situated in a long, shallow valley some 5 kilometres (3 miles wide) and bordered by low hills.

The valley is on average 3,750 metres above sea level, the city higher still. If you climb that high, the slightest effort leaves you breathless. We couldn't duplicate Tiahuanaco today without issuing oxygen equipment to the workmen. Yet the ancient peoples of the district managed to transport thousands of tonnes of stone to that great height at a time before the wheel was invented in South America or the horse introduced.

There are throughout the world a great many surviving structures that prove the people of the ancient world had far more efficient methods of moving stone than we do today – but nowhere, including Egypt, is there a more impressive example of their skills than at Baalbek in Lebanon.

Baalbek means City of the Sun in Arabic, a direct translation of the name Heliopolis, which is what it was called when it came under Egyptian rule around 323 BC. The Romans moved in about 64 BC and left the extensive ruins you can still see today some 1,200 metres above sea level in the Lebanese Mountains. Among the ruins are the remains of two huge temples.

Although Europeans started to take note of those temples as long ago as the 16th Century, it wasn't until 1898 that anybody started excavating them. From then until 1903, a German archaeological expedition worked to unearth their secrets. What they found was extraordinary.

All the buildings in the temple complex stood on a

raised platform enclosed by a massive retaining wall. This wall contains three of the largest cut stones ever used in any building anywhere. All three are over 4 metres high and more than 3 metres thick. The first is 19 metres long. The second has a length of 19 metres. The third, at 19.5 metres, is longer still. Each one is estimated to weigh around 1,000 tonnes. All three were raised to a height of 8 metres in order to rest on the lower courses of the wall.

It appears the Romans didn't raise these giants, but simply erected their own structures on foundations that were already there. Since nothing much is known about Baalbek prior to a few hundred years BC, nobody has the least idea of when the foundations were laid, or who laid them.

Baalbek

But what is known is the quarry from which the stones were cut. It lies over 1 kilometre ($3/4$ of a mile) from the temple site and in it lies a cut stone block so immense – it measures 21 metres x 4.2 metres x 4.5 metres and weighs in excess of 1,200 tonnes – that, like the stones in the temple, it could not be lifted today using the world's largest crane. Yet at some point in prehistory, our ancestors dragged stones this size half way up a mountain. Or did they?

Chapter 22

STONE MOVING WITHOUT TEARS

An old Arab legend insists the Big Sweaty Men Theory of stone moving is way off the mark, at least as far as building the pyramids was concerned. According to this story, what really happened was that a piece of magical papyrus (parchment) was placed underneath each stone. Then a priest came forward and struck the block with a special rod, causing it to glide forward 'the distance of a bow-shot.' In this way, even the heaviest granite slabs were transported with ease from faraway Aswan.

Once the stones reached Giza, priests 'sang' them up the stepped terraces of the pyramid as it gradually rose skywards. Workmen manhandled them into place, their job made easy by the fact that each block was now featherlight. This is hardly the sort of legend you'd rush to take seriously, were it not for the experience of an old friend of mine.

In 1961, Patricia ('Paddy') Slade's husband Peter decided he wanted to show her India where he'd been brought up and gone to school. The couple were stationed in Iraq at the time – Peter was in the Army – so they decided on an adventurous overland journey to their destination. Using a mix of Land Rovers, ponies and camels, they travelled through Uzbekistan before entering Pakistan by way of the Khyber Pass. They toured a little, then crossed the border and eventually ended up in Poona in India. A couple of days later, a friend mentioned a local religious ceremony that promised to be interesting.

It turned out to be the oddest religious ceremony either of them had ever seen. It took place in the open air and featured as its centrepiece an enormous lump of rock estimated to weigh some 40 tonnes. When the participants had gathered, 11 white-robed priests appeared and began to circle the stone while chanting.

After the 11 priests had circled the stone 11 times, one of them gave a signal. At once all chanting and movement stopped. Each priest placed a fingertip on the rock and suddenly lifted it shoulder high. After holding it aloft for 20 seconds, they gently set it down again.

When something as incredible as this happens, your immediate thought is trickery. But then the priests

ATLANTIS

asked for volunteers who might be interested in lifting the stone for themselves. Paddy Slade stepped forward at once.

Along with a small group from the audience, she was instructed how to chant in the same way as the priests, then told to circle the stone. At a signal from the priests, everyone was required to place a single finger on the boulder and try to lift it. They did so and the 40 tonnes of stone shot up as easily as it had before. Paddy believes the sound of their chanting somehow affected its weight.

The idea that sound can somehow influence the weight of stone is supported by an extraordinary report brought back by a Swedish doctor from a trip to Tibet in the early 1930s. The doctor, who protected his identity under the name of 'Jarl', was invited by a Tibetan friend to stay in a monastery southwest of the capital, Lhasa. While he was there, the lamas (priests) took him to watch one of the monastery's more interesting construction projects.

Work was underway at a cave in a cliff face, more than 210 metres above ground level. In front of the cave was a broad ledge and on this ledge the monks were engaged in building a stone wall. To reach the ledge, each man had to climb down stout ropes hung from the top of the cliff. There was no indication at all of how they got the stones up. But Jarl was soon to find out.

STONE MOVING WITHOUT TEARS

At ground level there was a large group of monks from the monastery, some of whom were carrying massive drums and trumpets. Embedded in the ground roughly 210 metres away from the cliff face – i.e. much the same distance from the cliff as the cave was above ground – was a large, flat, bowl-shaped stone. As Jarl watched, a monk with a knotted length of rope began to measure out distances and place instruments and people in position.

First of all, 13 drums and six trumpets were carefully arranged in a 90° arc around the bowl-stone. Then lines of eight or ten monks were asked to stand behind each instrument. Three further monks were moved to the centre of the arc. The one in the middle was equipped with a small drum slung from a leather strap around his neck. The two flanking monks stood behind much larger drums hanging from stout wooden frames.

Next the first of the trumpeters were put in place, one on either side of the monks with the large drums. Each trumpet was a monster about 3 metres long. Beside them came more monks with drums hung in frames, including two of the largest Jarl had ever seen. Beyond them, completing the arc, were alternating placements of drums and trumpets, finishing up with two large drums. Jarl noted the fact that every drum he could see was open at one end, and this end was always pointed towards the bowl-stone.

When the monks and their instruments were all in position, measured out by the knotted rope, a yak-drawn sled appeared. On it was a large stone block, some 1 metre by 1 metre by 1.3 metres. Monks manhandled it from the sled into the depression on the bowl-stone. Then, as these monks scuttled clear, an astonishing process got underway. The monk with the small drum at the centre of the arc began a rhythmic chant. After a moment he took up the rhythm on his drum. Despite its small size, the sound it made was so sharp and penetrating that it actually hurt Jarl's ears.

It seemed as though the small drum was being used as a timekeeper, for the beat was taken up by the trumpets which produced a low, deep pulse, then the remainder of the drums, which the monks beat with leather-headed sticks.

The sound reverberated across the surrounding mountains, growing so loud that the ground itself seemed to vibrate. For three or four minutes, nothing else happened, then the stone block in the centre of the bowl stone suddenly shivered, then wobbled visibly, although nobody was touching it.

At once, the monks began to tilt both their trumpets and drums slowly upwards. As Jarl watched, utterly bewildered, the stone block followed the movement of the instruments. It was impossible and yet the stone was levitating higher and higher above the bowl. The deep rhythm of trumpet and drum continued without pause. The stone block began to move faster, then abruptly sped off in an arc towards the cave mouth high above in the cliff face.

As the stone hovered above the ledge, the monks cut off the sound. The stone crashed down in a spray of dust and gravel and the monks on the ledge began to manhandle it into their wall.

Many Tibetan secrets were lost when the Chinese invaded their country in 1950 and it seems the use of sound to influence weight was definitely among them. Twenty years before the invasion, an Austrian filmmaker reported being shown two curious artefacts of Tibetan origin. One was a golden gong, ringed with iron and brass. The other was a stringed instrument, rather like an open lute without the fret, made from a metal bowl and supported in a sturdy wooden frame.

The two implements were used together. Two large screens were set up in a V-shape to reflect sound and the instruments placed in front of them. When the gong was struck, it produced a dull, dead sound that set up a sympathetic vibration in the strings of the bowl.

Once the vibrations got going properly, the sound produced could be directed by means of the screens. The monk who was demonstrating the instruments beamed it towards a large stone block. When this was done, the filmmaker found to his astonishment he could lift the stone with one hand. Without the sound, it was completely immovable.

The monk told him that in ancient times instruments of this sort had been used to build defensive walls around the whole of Tibet. Since Jarl, the Swedish doctor, discovered the Tibetans could lift up to six large blocks in an hour using their trumpets and drums, this does not seem a bizarre claim – and strongly supports the notion that our distant ancestors knew a lot more about stone moving than we do today.

Chapter 23
PREHISTORIC CITY

Moving stone is one thing, but knowing what to do with it is quite another. Can we really be expected to believe the grunting cavemen of our prehistoric textbooks were actually skilled engineers? It seems we can. Although the writers of our textbooks somehow haven't noticed, there is more hard evidence of large scale prehistoric engineering works than for everything else Plato wrote about put together.

We might usefully start with a place we visited just a couple of chapters ago – the Bolivian city of Tiahuanaco, with the Sun Temple the size of Trafalgar Square.

Judging by what remains, Tiahuanaco was a sophisticated city. The famous explorer Thor Heyerdahl referred to it a few years ago as 'the mightiest ruins in South America.' The Spanish conquistadors who found

ATLANTIS

it wandered open-mouthed through large empty spaces bounded by vertical stone walls, some carved as huge single pieces with perfect angles. They discovered a high pyramid-shaped mound and depictions of standing human figures cut into enormous blocks of stone incised with delicate patterns.

Among many free-standing gateways was the imposing Gateway of the Sun, which featured various decorative motifs and carved reliefs of a figure in a sunburst headdress holding a serpent staff. Around him were winged human and bird-headed figures. Beneath him were 12 heads, also with sunburst headdresses, linked together by a celestial serpent.

More recent visits by archaeologists have defined six beautifully designed architectural complexes and there is strong evidence to suggest the site may once have been much larger than the part that remains visible today. The city was extraordinarily well built. One modern visitor wrote:

> The walls were put together from megaliths, titanic many-sided stones, accurately cut and ground to a smooth finish, then fitted so precisely that no mortar is needed to bind them. There are no chinks in the walls. I couldn't even pound a chisel between the rocks. I measured a medium sized block. It was twenty feet by ten by three (7 metres by 3 metres by 1 metre). This figured out at around fifty tons ... for it was hard Andean granite like most of the blocks ...Each

> block in these walls is notched so that it interlocks tightly with the stone underneath it, as well as with its neighbours on each side.

If you consult your textbooks, they'll tell you this mighty city was built around 150 BC, with a nod to the possibility that it might have been earlier – just possibly dating to 2200 BC – or later by as much as AD 800. But one archaeologist – and the entire Bolivian Government – decided that even the 2200 BC date was ridiculously recent.

Arthur Posnansky studied Tiahuanaco for more than 30 years. One of the things he discovered was that its builders had a great knowledge of astronomy. (Those 'decorative motifs' on the Gateway of the Sun are actually a planetary calendar.) An extensive structure known as the Kalasasaya ('Standing Pillars') had, he believed been used as an astronomical observatory.

ATLANTIS

After taking careful measurements of the Kalasasaya, he was able to determine the prime observation points and solstice indicators. The summer and winter solstices mark turning points of the year – the longest and shortest days – and have always been hugely important to farming communities.

By comparing the ancient markers with the solstice points today, Posnansky was able to calculate when the Kalasasaya was built. At first he couldn't believe his figures, but when he checked and rechecked, they still came out the same. According to these findings, the Kalasasaya had been laid out as an observatory around 15000 BC.

Posnansky's report on his findings was studied, accepted and endorsed by the Bolivian Government, but Posnansky's fellow academics weren't so sure. They decided, by and large, that the Kalasasaya really was an observatory (which is how it's now usually described in the textbooks) but that when it came to dating, Posnansky was talking through his hat.

All the same, the German Astronomical Commission sent an expedition to check it out. After two years of careful investigation, the astronomers of the expedition announced four possible dates for the building of Tiahuanaco. The most recent was 4000 BC. The others were 9300 BC, 10000 BC and Posnansky's original 15000 BC.

Since you won't find much discussion of these

possibilities in your school books, I'd like to point out that all but the most recent of these dates would place Tiahuanaco firmly in the depths of the supposed Ice Age at the same time as Atlantis.

But can we seriously believe this astonishing city could possibly be so old? You're going to have to make up your own mind about that, but before you do, there's something you should know.

Tiahuanaco was a port. Its extensive harbours, docks, quays and wharves are visible to this day. Yet this port is 3,962 metres above sea level and a very long way from the nearest water. When the fact was first discovered, it made so little sense that historians decided Tiahuanaco must have been built as a ceremonial city, used only for symbolic rituals. (The theory also solved the problem of how residents of Tiahuanaco lived and worked in an environment where they could hardly breathe.)

But then archaeological finds made in 1995 showed Tiahuanaco was once the capital of an empire that extended across eastern and southern Bolivia, north-western Argentina, northern Chile, and southern Peru. So it was definitely a working city, yet one constructed as a port when it is clearly nothing of the sort.

There is a solution to this puzzle, but it's a solution so incredible that it has been firmly banned from your textbooks. The Bolivian Altiplano on which Tiahuanaco stands high in the Andes Mountains, is the highest lake basin in the world. There are three lakes on the Altiplano and all of them contain salt water. The area is also noted for its salt marshes and dry salt beds so great they are classified as salt deserts. Groundwater feeding into the lakes passes over rock that doesn't yield salt. So the question is, where did all that salt come from? The answer is the sea.

If you take a pick and shovel to the Andes Mountains, you'll find a 480 kilometre (300 mile) long layer of whitish material at a height of more than 3,500 metres. Scientists will tell you it's the remains of *marine* plants. This indicates that at some time in the past, these great mountains pushed up out of the sea. A site called the Giant's Field in the eastern Andes has yielded up fossil bones of mastodons, huge elephant-like animals that were extinct by 8000 BC. These creatures required vast quantities of vegetation for food and could not have survived on a high, barren plateau. Their natural habitat was coastal marsh. This indicates that at some time prior to 8000 BC, the area was at sea level.

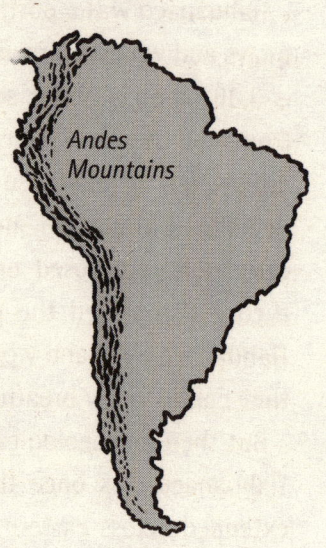

Geological evidence shows without a doubt that the

Tiahuanaco Altiplano itself was once underwater, drowned by an inland sea stretching more than 720 kilometres (450 miles).

Put all this together and you get a picture of the Altiplano rising from the sea bed at some point in the past and gradually draining to form its present landscape. The building of Tiahuanaco when the Altiplano was still at sea level would make a lot more sense than it does today. The city could have functioned as a port. Transporting the stones would have been simpler and the building work would have been a whole lot easier.

When the city was constructed, it would have been set in a fertile area and enjoyed a pleasant climate, thus solving the problem of how its citizens survived and were fed. But if Tiahuanaco really was built before the mountains rose, the evidence of the Giant's Field fossils shows we must be looking at a time period before the mastodons became extinct.

Which puts Tiahuanaco firmly in the time period of Atlantis.

Chapter 24

MORE PREHISTORIC CITIES

Tiahuanaco isn't the only prehistoric city. Back in 1940, two archaeologists began work on a Stone Age site near Ipiutak in the Arctic Circle. They expected to find the usual bone or flint arrowheads, possibly a primitive pot fragment or two. What they actually found was mind numbing.

First they uncovered the remains of a well-built house. Then another and another. By the time the total reached ten, they realised they had stumbled on an ancient hamlet. As it climbed to 50, they amended their conclusion: they were definitely dealing with an ancient village.

Then the 50 turned to 100 ... 200. Incredibly, they were digging up a Stone Age town. Except they weren't. By the time they uncovered the remains of

MORE PREHISTORIC CITIES

some 600 – with indications that at least a further 200 remained to be excavated – they were forced to admit they had stumbled on a prehistoric city.

The city stretched for more than 1.5 kilometres (1 mile). It was laid out on a logical grid, exactly like modern American cities such as New York or Washington. Artefacts and craft work discovered on the site were, the archaeologists reported, of 'elaborate and sophisticated carving and ... beautiful workmanship'.

There are indications of another prehistoric city on the Pacific island of Ponape. According to a report to the Royal Geographical Society:

> A massive breakwater runs along the edge of the ... sea. Out to sea lie other islands, where there are scattered remains of another ancient sea wall. The most remarkable ... ruins are on the Islet Tanack. The water front is filled with a solid line of massive stonework about six feet wide (2 metres) and six feet above the shallow waterway. Above this is a striking example of immensely solid cyclopean masonry (ancient stonework made from gigantic,

ATLANTIS

> irregular blocks) – a great wall twenty feet (nearly 7 metres high) and ten feet (over 3 metres) thick.

The report goes on to tell of various areas walled to a height of 12 metres and a massive underground vault roofed with enormous slabs of basalt. More evidence of prehistoric city building comes from Sri Lanka, a large island off the coast of India. Although the official history of Sri Lanka claims that before an Indian invasion in the 6th Century BC only a few nomadic hunter-gatherers lived there, British excavations in the late 19th Century unearthed a prehistoric fortress which used massive stone blocks 5.5 metres by 2 metres by 70 centimetres. Something of this scale was clearly not built by primitive nomads. Nor were they likely to have built the currently unexcavated city of Vijithapura which aerial survey shows to extend over 100 hectares.

Some prehistoric cities have been incorporated into more recent building projects and are consequently wrongly dated in modern textbooks. Two cases in point are Cuzco and Machu Picchu. Cuzco, in southern Peru, was the capital of the Inca empire from the 14th Century until the Spanish conquest. It was designed in the shape of a puma and two rivers were actually straightened to form its tail. Today it is visited by tourists who goggle at enormous cut-stone blocks so perfectly laid that no mortar was ever needed between them.

Local histories claim it was built by a king named Pachacuti who reigned between 1440 and 1470 AD. But this seems unlikely – the city is far too big to have been completed in the time.

Archaeologists are slowly coming to believe the Incas simply added to an already existing site. There are clear examples of two distinct architectural styles in the city – the astounding megalithic structures and the much less impressive Inca buildings made with smaller stones and using mortar.

The same pattern can be seen at Machu Picchu, spectacularly set on a high precipice 2400 metres above sea level about 80 kilometres (50 miles) northwest of Cuzco. The American explorer who discovered it remarked that the remains of its buildings showed standards 'as fine as the finest stonework in the world.

Like Cuzco, Machu Picchu is a mix of architectural styles. Some buildings are made from small stones held together with mortar, but the most impressive structures feature the type of great notched megaliths found at Tiahuanaco. These are so finely placed that you couldn't slip a playing card between them. The Incas had no idea how to handle stones of this size. One of the Spanish chroniclers watched what happened when an Inca mason decided to use one of the original megaliths in his own fortifications.

Ropes were attached to the stone and 20,000 Incas attempted to drag it to the new fortifications. The first time they reached a slope they lost control of the stone, which rolled back down, killing thousands of them. Interestingly, while Machu Picchu was laid out with the agricultural terraces of a city, the Incas never lived there – they used it purely as a ceremonial site. Dr Rolf Müller, an astronomer who worked with Posnansky at Tiahuanaco, reported that he'd made measurements to show parts of both Cuzco and Machu Picchu were lined up to point to the ancient positions of certain stars. This proved the cities were far older than the establishment of the Inca Empire. He suggested that the huge megaliths might be the same age as those of Tiahuanaco.

If you take the trouble to look, the remains of prehistoric cities lie scattered right across the face of the globe. Sometimes they are known only to those who live in the immediate area, sometimes they are excavated and reported. Yet they continue to be ignored by those who decide what you should know about the whole broad sweep of human prehistory.

Did anybody ever tell you about the ancient ruins on the site of Kevkenes Dagh in Asia Minor? It is a great isolated city, built by an entirely unknown culture. High walled fortifications, from 4 metres to 4.5 metres thick, enclosed an area of 2.5 kilometres (1.5 miles) by 1.6 kilometres (1 mile). Its discovery was reported in the *Geographical Review* as long ago as 1928 ... then quietly forgotten.

ATLANTIS

A few years ago, Irish archaeologists discovered the remains of a prehistoric metropolis on top of a hill near Baltinglass in County Wicklow. I heard about the site because I happened to be living nearby at the time, but I doubt it's going to change the picture of the shambling caveman they keep putting out. And what about the reports of city ruins, temples and monuments hidden in the wooded valleys stretching along the coastline through Honduras up to Yucatan in Central America? The remains were described as superbly carved monoliths and stones of immense size covered with ornaments and inscriptions reminiscent of Egyptian, Indian and even Chinese art. An article in *Pan-American Magazine* suggested they might be the remnants of Atlantis.

Chapter 25

PREHISTORIC ENGINEERING

The Great Pyramid of Egypt (which, you'll recall, is something we could scarcely build today) covers over 5 hectares (13 acres) of bedrock. Two and a half million limestone and granite blocks went into its construction, each weighing between two and 70 tonnes. It rises over 201 tiers to the height of a modern 40-storey building.

In its original form, the exterior was covered by 15-tonne slabs of polished limestone giving a total mass of 6,300,000 tonnes. To put it into context, that's more stone than in all the cathedrals and churches built in England for the past 2,000 years. Napoleon once calculated that by tearing down the pyramid he would have enough raw material to erect a wall 3 metres high and 1 metre thick around the whole of France.

ATLANTIS

You'd imagine this incredible structure would have to be the largest pyramid on Earth. But it isn't. The largest pyramid on Earth is located in the Qin Ling Shan mountains of Tibet, about 100 kilometres (62 miles) southwest of the city of Xi'an, in the People's Republic of China. It stands 300 metres high and was built, according to records stored in a local Buddhist monastery, in the depths of prehistory.

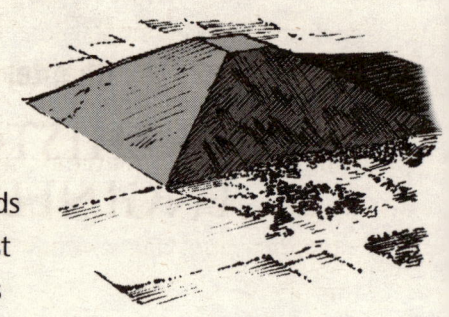

The Great Pyramid of China is not the only example of a large-scale engineering project carried out in what we have been told was the frozen depths of the Ice Age.

Evidence of sophisticated engineering skills in prehistoric Sri Lanka arose when the Gal Oya Dam Project got underway in the 1950s. As work started, earth-moving machinery quickly hit on the remnants of an ancient dam at exactly the same spot. When this was operating, it had regulated the distribution of billions of litres of water through a series of artificial lakes. There was more than 9.5 kilometres (6 miles) of sluices and tunnelling 10 metres high constructed from 15 tonne stone blocks.

An even bigger prehistoric dam turned up in

PREHISTORIC ENGINEERING

America. It was discovered in 1892 when surveyors were working to establish the boundary line between the United States and Mexico. The dam stretched for nearly 9.5 kilometres (6 miles) in the Animas Valley of New Mexico and when it was first built would have enclosed a reservoir 8 kilometres (5 miles) long and over half a kilometre wide, holding water to a depth of almost 7 metres. Engineers estimated 8 to 10 million cubic metres of material must have been moved to create the structure. There were traces of two more enormous dams within 13 kilometres (8 miles) of this one.

America is actually littered with incredible examples of prehistoric engineering. There's a well planned series of earthworks covering an area 2.5 square kilometres (1 mile square) in the Florida Everglades near Lake Okechobee. The site includes a platform 9 metres high and 76 metres long and the structures are laid out with mathematical precision. There are stone fortifications, using blocks weighing up to a tonne, running through the Berkeley and Oakland Hills.

There's an artificial mound near Cahokia, Illinois, that's over 300 metres long, more than 200 metres wide, and is still to this day over 30 metres high. There's a stone fort with walls 2.5 metres thick near Massie's Creek in Ohio. The stones of its gateways have fused together as if subjected to intense heat. (Fused stone is also seen in some prehistoric forts on the west coast of Scotland. The textbooks claim they must have been struck by lightning, but actually only industrial lasers could generate enough heat to melt stone.)

There are massive irrigation canals at Pueblo Grande, Arizona. Two of them are particularly big – 26 and 18 metres wide from crest to crest. They extend for at least 11 kilometres (7 miles) in one case, 14 kilometres (9 miles) in the other. Despite their obvious importance, they have yet to be excavated so their full extent is unknown.

There is an 80 kilometre (50 mile) stretch of prehistoric wall in Peru. Today it's a ruined stone structure that varies from 4 to 5 metres in width, and is up to 5 metres high. There are 14 forts along its length, some covering an area of 60 metres by 90 metres with stone walls 5 metres high and nearly 2 metres thick.

One of the earliest of all Britain's many prehistoric monuments is an earthwork enclosure known as the Dorset Cursus. The enclosure is bounded by parallel earthen banks beyond which ditches have been dug. The Cursus, which meanders near the Dorset-Wiltshire border across the downs of Cranborne Chase, is 9.5 kilometres (6 miles) long and contains a land area of 90 hectares (220 acres). Some 185,000 cubic metres of earth had to be moved to build it.

An elaborate network of prehistoric earthwork fortifications has been discovered in East Africa. One of the forts has a circumference falling just short of

PREHISTORIC ENGINEERING

5 kilometres (3 miles). In Zambia, there is evidence that prehistoric miners somehow managed to cut into a cliff face at a height of over 150 metres. Their workings were over 7.5 metres wide and 7 metres high. They appeared to be mining manganese and haematite. Haematite is the main source of iron. Manganese is today used in many alloys – notably steel – to improve strength and hardness. Carbon dating of charcoal samples from the site showed the work was taking place more than 28,000 years ago.

In France, prehistoric engineering abilities reached such a degree of precision that larger-than-life fingerprints have been etched into megaliths on the Ile de Gavr'inis, Brittany.

The patterns recorded are similar to those kept on modern police files and two of the megaliths display partial hand-prints.

There are paved prehistoric roads in Yucatan, New Zealand, Kenya and Malta.

There is a prehistoric water tank in Sri Lanka with a surface area equivalent to Lake Geneva.

There are 27,000 kilometres (170,000 miles) of underground aqueducts in Iran.

These finds, which once again represent only a tiny fragment of the overall evidence available, indicate that our prehistoric ancestors were perfectly capable of carrying out even the most elaborate of the engineering feats Plato wrote about when he described Atlantis. But could they, as he claimed, really have navigated the world's oceans?

Chapter 26

PREHISTORIC NAVIGATORS

According to the textbooks, the earliest sailors never ventured far from home, mainly because they didn't really know how to get back again. They crawled along the coast to sail from port to port, or hopped from one island to another. Essentially what they were doing was to memorise a set of landmarks between the start of their voyage and their destination. It wasn't a system that would take you very far.

A few hardy sailors ventured further, however, and with luck, good judgement and a growing knowledge of local wind patterns, managed fairly lengthy voyages. By about 2500 BC, for example, there was a well-worn trade route between Egypt and the island of Crete, a distance of 80 kilometres (300 miles). With a

ATLANTIS

favourable wind, you could make the voyage in about five days.

This was as far as anybody went at the time, but then, approximately 1,500 years later, the Phoenicians, who were notable merchants, traders, and colonizers of the Mediterranean in the first millennium BC, discovered the Pole Star.

The thing about the Pole Star is that it doesn't move. (Because of the Earth's rotation, other stars appear to move around it.) If you sail directly towards it, you can be sure you're sailing north. It sounds like a simple discovery, but it enabled the Phoenicians to boldly go where no man had gone before – and pick up some very valuable knowledge of winds and currents on the way.

Somewhere between 610 and 595 BC, Phoenician mariners managed to sail right around Africa on the orders of an Egyptian pharaoh. A little later, Carthaginian sailors from North Africa somehow managed to reach the Azores, a group of islands in the North Atlantic, but that was probably luck more than anything else.

Longer and longer routes were eventually established. In about AD 400, for example, Polynesian navigators made a 3,700-kilometre (2,300-mile) voyage across the open Pacific to reach Hawaii. Sometime before the 10th Century, Irish seafarers hopped via the Shetland Islands and the Faeroe Islands

PREHISTORIC NAVIGATORS

as far as Iceland. The Vikings subsequently made it as far as North America and in the 16th Century, an expedition led by Ferdinand Magellan finally managed to sail right around the world.

From all of this, you can see the textbooks claim that nobody, but nobody, engaged in deep-ocean navigation any earlier than 600 BC – and even that date was probably a fluke. Serious voyaging really only started about 500 years ago. But this cosy picture ignores some very interesting evidence.

Look up Pitcairn Island. Your books will tell you that it's a tiny volcanic island 2,172 kilometres (1,350 miles) south-east of Tahiti in the Pacific Ocean, famed for the fact that it's now entirely populated by survivors of a mutiny on the *HMS Bounty* in 1789. So far the information is correct. But your textbooks will probably add that Pitcairn was first discovered in 1767. That date is nonsense. If you are mutinous enough to travel to Pitcairn yourself, you'll find a rock inscription there that reads:

> Our crew, wrecked in a storm, made land, thank God. We are people from the Manu region. We worship Ra in accordance with the scripture We behold the sun and give voice.

At least, that's how it reads in translation. The inscription itself is written in the Libyan dialect of Ancient Egyptian.

The remains of some very large boats have been unearthed by Egyptologists, including several that date to the building of the Giza pyramids. But since the experts are locked into the idea that nobody went ocean sailing before 600 BC, the textbooks will tell you these ships only travelled up and down the Nile. Their immense size is explained by suggesting they must have been used for ceremonial purposes. Like so much else in your textbooks, that theory is nonsense too.

An Egyptian scarab, symbol of good luck, was dug up in a cane field at Hambledon, Australia, in the early 1900s. At much the same time, a farmer digging west of Cairns (also in Australia) came across an Egyptian coin. Next thing you know, they'd found a hieroglyphic inscription 80.5 kilometres (50 miles) south of Sydney. This was enough to convince Professor R. Gilroy of the Mount York History Museum that the Ancient Egyptians must have visited Australia. I find it pretty persuasive too.

If they really did get to Australia, there's some

evidence to suggest they made it as far as New Zealand as well. Ornamental designs discovered on some of the oldest Egyptian mummies, have their counterparts in the traditional patterns of the Maori culture. What's more, Maori women often have chin tattoos identical to those worn by women of Upper Egypt.

All the same, the civilisation of Ancient Egypt is dated to a much later period than the fall of Atlantis. So even if the Egyptians did sail the oceans of the world, it doesn't prove that anyone was out there earlier. For that you need to read the works of Charles Hapgood. Professor Hapgood taught the history of science at Keene State College in New Hampshire, U.S.A. He was an academic who was well thought of – Einstein himself endorsed one of his early books – but he had some very peculiar ideas.

He went on record, for example, with the theory that long before the emergence of Sumeria, Egypt, Greece and Rome – right back in the depths of prehistory, in fact – there existed a major civilisation far more advanced than any of them. Indeed, he believed it was more advanced than anything the world knew before the 18th Century. It was advanced in astronomy, navigation, mathematics, map making and ship building. Its mathematicians were capable of calculating the exact length of the solar year to a tolerance of two seconds. Its geographers had accurately measured the circumference of the Earth.

ATLANTIS

Its astronomers knew about the moons of Jupiter and the satellites of Saturn.

The prehistoric civilisation had trade links that were literally worldwide. It had an organised government and a strong economy. And its most impressive skills were those of navigation. Prehistoric sailors knew how to calculate degrees of longitude, which measures your position east or west anywhere on the globe and was something only achieved by our own culture in the 18th Century. They explored the Arctic and Antarctic, which we only managed in the 19th Century.

Nowhere did Professor Hapgood say this prehistoric civilisation was actually Atlantis. But you can see the similarities.

Chapter 27

MARVELLOUS MAPS

Professor Hapgood didn't just pull his ideas out of a hat. Where he got them – and the proof to back them – is a longish story, but sort of interesting.

It started back in 1929 when somebody came across an old map that had lain for years in the Topkapi Palace Museum in Istanbul, Turkey. The map dated back to the year 919 in the Muslim calendar, which meant it was drawn up in AD 1513. It originally belonged to a Turkish Admiral (*Piri*) named Re'is. He may have been called 'Admiral' but Piri Re'is was a pirate.

Having found the map, the Museum deposited a copy in the American Library of Congress, then forgot about it. A Turkish naval officer made his own copy and presented that to the United States Hydrographic Office. After which nothing happened for 27 years. Then, in 1956, a professional mapmaker named

ATLANTIS

M. I. Walters came across the Hydrographic Office copy and things started moving.

You need to put this in context. Most early 16th Century maps are pretty batty. They have areas marked 'Here be dragons' and where the mapmaker didn't know a stretch of coastline, he felt free to make it up. You might wonder how sailors got anywhere with maps like these and the answer is they didn't. If you went on a voyage in the early 1500s, you took your life in your hands and there was a very good chance you'd drop it.

But the Piri Re'is map was something else. It was drawn with a degree of accuracy that was little short of astonishing. The outline of South America was correct, for example, even though the continent had only been discovered 13 years earlier and not yet accurately surveyed.

And there were things about the map that moved beyond astonishing to the positively creepy. The longitudes of a whole range of countries from Morocco to North Africa's Ivory Coast were accurately depicted, even though nobody knew how to calculate

MARVELLOUS MAPS

longitude correctly for more than 200 years after Piri Re'is was dead. The continent of Antarctica was right there for everybody to see ... despite the fact Antarctica wasn't discovered until 1818. Spookiest of all was the map's depiction of the Mid-Atlantic Ridge. You can only detect that using sonar.

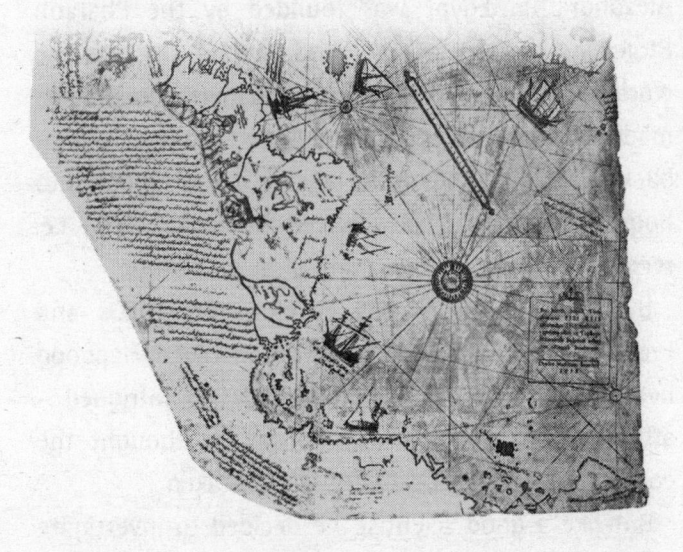

All this was shocking enough, but it was about to get worse. Walters loaned the map to a friend of his called Alington H. Mallery, an elderly navigator who spent his retirement studying old maps. Mallery discovered the Antarctic had been drawn not as it is today, but as it was thousands of years ago *before it was covered by ice.*

It turned out that Piri Re'is hadn't drawn up the map himself, but had copied it from 20 other maps. One of

ATLANTIS

these was the work of Christopher Columbus, the Italian navigator usually credited (quite wrongly) with having discovered America. The other 19 had been rescued from the Library of Alexandria when it was destroyed by Arab invaders in AD 640

That's a particularly interesting source. The Library of Alexandria in Egypt was founded by the Pharaoh Ptolemy I (c. 367-283 BC) and quickly became the world's foremost collection of papyri (documents made of papyrus reeds), tablets and artefact dating back to ancient times. In its heyday, it was supposed to house material that had survived the Great Flood – i.e. records of times we now think of as prehistoric.

By now our story has entered the 1960s and Professor Hapgood is about to get involved. Hapgood heard about Mallery's findings and was intrigued – although it's probably true to say he thought the conclusions were almost certainly mistaken.

But like a good scientist, he decided to investigate with an open mind. To that end, he set a group of his students the task of studying a whole collection of ancient maps, including portolans (old books of sailing directions with charts, descriptions of harbours, etc) and the controversial Piri Re'is map.

What they discovered was entirely unexpected. First of all, the mediaeval portolans proved far too accurate for the time they were in use. Many of them were just as accurate as modern charts and some showed features, like the island of Cuba, that simply hadn't been discovered in the Middle Ages.

Then there was a Chinese map, cut in stone around AD 1137, that showed similar features to the portolans, indicating the growing map mystery might well be a worldwide phenomenon.

When the students started to examine the Piri Re'is map, the mystery deepened alarmingly. As Piri Re'is himself claimed, the document was a combination of 20 different sources, but the pirate 'Admiral' had done a very sloppy job of it. He'd left out huge stretches of coastline and shown the Amazon river twice.

Sloppy or not, it was clear that Re'is had followed the ancient custom of drawing his map from a centre chosen at random. But surprisingly, the centre in this case lay off the map itself. The students made a few calculations and discovered that even though it wasn't shown, the Piri Re'is map was centred on a place called Syene, which lies on the River Nile in Egypt. If you're curious, you can still find it on modern maps, very close to Aswan.

Syene sets alarm bells ringing for students of history. It was, in fact, a very important place in ancient times, when it was used to figure out the exact moment of the summer and winter solstices, when the sun reached its furthest point north or south of the equator. (On June 21 and December 22 at noon, each year the solstice sun reflected in the village well.)

ATLANTIS

Since this meant that Syene was in a direct line between the Sun and the Earth's centre, a clever Greek named Eratosthenes used it to calculate the size of our planet.

He didn't do too badly and his findings were put to good use in drawing up Ancient Greek maps. But the maps weren't quite right because Eratosthenes' calculations were just a little bit off. Every Greek map made at this time contained exactly the same error. In fact, you could tell it was a Greek map just by looking for the error.

And the exact same error shows up in the Piri Re'is map. Which meant it had to be a copy of one or more Greek originals. Unfortunately that discovery didn't solve the mystery. We know a great deal about the Ancient Greeks – who left us written records – and they definitely weren't great ocean sailors. Most of their voyages never got past the Mediterranean. So they shouldn't have known about the places that appeared on the Piri Re'is map either.

But if the Greek maps Piri Re'is copied weren't made from the observations of Greek sailors, they must have been copied too. And since nobody else was making better maps than the Greeks at that time, they must have been copied from an *even earlier* source.

At this point in his reasoning, Hapgood did something amazing. He redrew the Piri Re'is map according to modern measurements for the size of the globe. This should have made it a lot less accurate, but it didn't. In fact, the various countries shown fell into place perfectly.

There was only one way this could have happened. Sometime before the rise of Ancient Greece there were sailors on the oceans of the Earth exploring and mapping vast areas of the globe. They knew how to build ships that would withstand Atlantic storms. They knew how to calculate latitude and longitude so they could find their way home from unknown seas.

These were no primitive prehistoric cavemen. They had to come from a forgotten civilisation.

Chapter 28

PREHISTORIC CIVILISATION

The Greek maps Piri Re'is copied from must have been drawn up sometime after the 3rd Century BC, because that's the time Eratosthenes made his famous error. But all that tells us is the Greeks must have copied from maps drawn up sometime before then, a stretch of history that runs from 200 BC to 4.5 billion BC, the time we think the Earth solidified.

Professor Hapgood went back to the claim by Captain Mallery that Piri Re'is had mapped an ice-free Antarctica. A little work confirmed this was actually the case – and Piri Re'is wasn't the only one. A map-maker named Oronteus Finaeus created a map in 1531 that also showed Antarctica free of ice and actually marked the position of the South Pole. This is, to say the least, peculiar. The only reason we know the outline

PREHISTORIC CIVILISATION

on these maps is accurate is that a scientific expedition took depth soundings across the Antarctic in 1949.

So how did the ancient mariners know what the continent looked like underneath all that ice? There are only two possible answers. One is that they were at least as technically sophisticated as we are today. The other is that they mapped the Antarctic before the ice formed.

Oronteus Finaeus' map

But of those two possibilities, only one really makes sense. The Antarctic has had its present ice cap since about 4000 BC. If a technically advanced civilisation with worldwide trade links was in place any time after that date, you can be certain we'd know about it. Such a civilisation would have existed at a time when we have a very clear picture of what the world was like and would, unless it was very shortlived, have overlapped the early civilisation of Sumer.

So we're left with a not-quite-so-technically-advanced civilisation that existed *before* 4000 BC. How much before?

Professor Hapgood went back to his maps. Some showed different sea levels – notably in the Aegean – than we have today. Some showed coastal contours that reflect the way Scotland and parts of Sweden were in the very distant past. One, a map once owned by someone named Hadji Ahmed in 1550, showed both the North Pole and a land bridge between Alaska and Siberia across the Bering Strait.

Putting all the evidence together indicated that the lost civilisation must have flourished earlier than 12000 BC. In a letter to a young librarian written in October, 1982, Hapgood claimed that in recent exciting discoveries he had convincing evidence of a whole cycle of civilisation suggesting advanced levels of science that might go back 100,000 years.

Professor Hapgood was knocked down and killed by a car before he could publish his convincing evidence.

Chapter 29
ANCIENT PYRAMIDS

The idea that civilisation might date back 100,000 years – to a time, that is, when your books assure you we'd only just come down from the trees – is so outlandish that you start to wonder if Professor Hapgood hadn't added in an extra zero by mistake. Even the oldest dating of Tiahuanaco (15000 BC) comes nowhere near that figure. All the same, there really is convincing evidence that civilised humanity walked this planet at a far earlier date than that.

Let's start with what's fast becoming a familiar structure in this book – the Great Pyramid at Giza in Egypt. Your textbooks will tell you this pyramid was built, as a tomb for the Pharaoh Khufu, somewhere around 2500 BC.

So confident is this statement that you might be forgiven for assuming that Egyptologists have

ATLANTIS

unearthed definite proof – written records, perhaps, or something that could be carbon dated. The reality is there are no hieroglyphics on or in the Great Pyramid, no carvings or decorations. There were no papyrus scrolls, no clay tablets, no writing of any sort found in its chambers. No mummy was ever discovered in this 'tomb', nor were any other human remains, ancient wood or the like, that could have been carbon dated.

The only hard evidence linking Khufu with this pyramid was a mason's mark discovered in the 19th Century by a British Guards Officer, Colonel (and later General) Richard Howard-Vyse ... and several experts think he faked it. In these circumstances, there is lots of room to doubt the dating.

Someone who doubts it hugely is the author/investigator Ralph Ellis, whose interest in the subject was sparked by a chance remark of his wife. While the couple were sightseeing at Giza, she asked him why there was a noticeable line running across one of the ancient pavements there.

To understand where this question led Ellis, you have to realise that the Great Pyramid you see in Egypt today is nothing like the Great Pyramid as it was originally built. At that time there was a highly polished limestone casing covering the entire structure. When it was new, the Great Pyramid gleamed white in the Egyptian sun.

The pyramid, casing stones and all, was erected on a paved foundation which stretched a little beyond the pyramid itself, framing the base. As you can imagine, the area of the pavement that wasn't actually under the pyramid has been subject to erosion over the ages. Sand, wind and tourist feet have all contributed to carry away a layer of its surface.

This process of erosion literally began the day the pyramid was built. It was very slow, very gradual, but if you waited long enough – several centuries perhaps – you would notice the result. The portion of the pavement underneath the pyramid didn't erode at all, of course. It was protected by the structure itself.

The beautiful white limestone casing stones of the Great Pyramid have all but disappeared today. They were stripped off by vandals about 1,000 years ago. Once they disappeared, you could see how they had protected the pavement underneath them. It was at a different, slightly higher, level than the pavement that had always been exposed; and the difference was marked by a clearly visible line – the same line Mrs Ellis spotted.

What occurred to Ralph Ellis in that *eureka* moment was that you should be able to use the rate of erosion to discover when the pyramid was actually built. He began to take measurements, not just at Giza, but at Dashur where there's another ancient pyramid.

At both sites he found the rate or erosion was 5 mm per 1,000 years, as shown by what had happened when the casing stones were removed. By applying this figure to the part of the pavement that had been eroding constantly since the beginning, he was able to calculate the ages of both pyramids.

The pyramid at Dashur was built around 8000 BC. The Great Pyramid at Giza was 30,000 years older.

Chapter 30

MEXICAN MYSTERY

Stone Erosion Dating makes logical sense, but it's a little too new to gain widespread acceptance. As a result, your textbooks will continue to assure you for the next few years that the Great Pyramid was built about 2500 BC – and that's quite understandable. What's less understandable is why they're still refusing to mention the findings of a Scots engineering professor and archaeologist, which make even Ralph Ellis's dating of the pyramids sound relatively recent.

William Niven, the professor in question, was a honorary life member of the American Museum of Natural History and various other scientific societies. He was fascinated by Mexico and began to explore it in 1889. By 1910, he'd taken a post as a mining engineer with a Mexican corporation but continued enthusiastically with his archaeological work. From then until 1930, he made a series of discoveries that would be ranked – if anybody had ever heard of them – among the most important in archaeological history.

The breakthrough came when he was excavating the ruined cities of Guerrero, southwest of Mexico City near Acapulco. As news of his activities spread, he began to get visits from local natives offering ancient artefacts – figurines and the like – for sale. They claimed the objects had been found at Mexico's well-known Teotihuacan ruins but Niven wasn't so sure. Eventually he bribed somebody to take him to the place the finds really came from.

This turned out to be a site just north of Mexico City which had been used as a source of building materials for centuries. As a result, several thousand enormous holes had been excavated over an area of about 518 square kilometres (200 square miles). To the local builders, they were nothing more than sand and clay pits. To Niven, however, they were an archaeological treasure trove.

As he examined the pits, he discovered the ground beneath his feet was layered in a very interesting way. First was 30 centimetres or so of earth, then 3 metres of boulders, gravel and sand which yielded up a great deal of broken pottery, clay figures, spearheads, arrowheads and beads of relatively recent origin.

Beneath this layer, more than 3 metres down, was the first really startling find – a concrete pavement.

MEXICAN MYSTERY

This floor seemed to be a man-made foundation of some sort, an indication that the area had been inhabited – and that the inhabitants had reached a high enough cultural level to make concrete. Underneath the pavement was another layer, approximately 2 metres deep, that contained only sand, gravel and small boulders.

Then came a second concrete pavement, as unexpected as the first. Below that, for about 5 metres, was another layer of boulders, gravel and sand on top of a thick layer of volcanic ash. Underneath the ash was a buried city.

The city was huge. Over a 20-year period of excavation, Niven discovered it stretched over more than 100 of the gravel pits without any indication that its outer boundary was in sight. It consisted of large, regular stone buildings, mortared with a white cement that was stronger than the stone itself. Most of the houses were ruined, crushed by the weight of earth on top of them, but one or two remained intact (although filled with volcanic ash). When these were excavated, Niven found abundant evidence of a sophisticated culture.

There were, for example, wall paintings that matched the very finest Greek and Egyptian art. One of them, a frieze that depicted the life of a shepherd, had been treated in such a way that its colours remained vibrant and fresh. In another chamber, Niven found an intact

ATLANTIS

goldsmith's workshop with 200 clay moulds. A floor tomb yielded up a copper axe and 125 terracotta figures, one of them cleverly constructed to allow its head to nod.

As he extended his excavations, Niven made an even more exciting find – the first of 2,600 stone tablets bearing a hitherto unknown – and still unreadable – pictographic script.

When Niven put all this evidence together, an almost incredible picture emerged. Beneath the sun-baked earth of Mexico there lay the ruins of three distinct cultures. Since sand and gravel layers are usually the result of flooding, each of the cultures appeared to have been overwhelmed by a series of tidal waves, separated by many thousands of years. The pattern of layering showed that between each cataclysm, hundreds, perhaps thousands of years went by during which there was no human life in the area at all.

One of the most intriguing aspects of Niven's find was that certain of the figurines and paintings showed Semitic, Phoenician and even Chinese features, suggesting worldwide trade links with the most ancient of the civilisations. Judging by the level at which he found it, Niven estimated the age of this culture at 50,000 years.

At about the time Niven was excavating his sand pits, another archaeologist, Dr Paul Felix Cabrera was digging up even more fabulous finds far to the south

MEXICAN MYSTERY

in Peru. These were a series of stone tablets which Cabrera also believed were at least 50,000 years old, despite the fact that some of them had accurate depictions of human internal anatomy while others showed sophisticated heart transplant operations.

Among the Cabrera tablets were a few that opened up even wilder possibilities concerning ancient civilisations and the length of time humanity has been on the planet. They showed engravings of men battling with dinosaurs – creatures that became extinct 65 *million* years ago.

Cabrera tablets

It's difficult to interpret finds like this, which may explain why so many scientists have chosen to ignore them. You can find dinosaur bones in any Natural History Museum and see wonderful artists' impressions of the creatures themselves in any bookshop. If it was produced today, an engraving of a man battling with a Tyrannosaurus Rex would be taken as a piece of fiction, like Stephen Spielberg's *Jurassic Park*.

But if Dr Cabrera is right in his estimate that the stone tablets are 50,000 years old, you have to ask yourself how the people of that time knew about dinosaurs. There are really only three possible answers to the question:

1. There was a civilisation 50,000 years ago that was just as advanced as we are – at least when it comes to investigating the ancient past.
2. Dinosaurs didn't *really* die out 65 million years ago. At least some of them hung on for another 64,950,000 years in order to bother our Mexican ancestors.
3. Humanity was on the planet at the same time as the dinosaurs and left records that were still being copied and preserved 50,000 years ago.

Today's scientists don't like any of these answers, but the one they like least of all is No. 3. According to evolutionary theory, not only were there no humans around at the time of the dinosaurs, there were no mammals of any sort around then either. By the time the dinosaurs died out (65,000,000 years ago) the only representative of the genus to which you and I belong was a thing the size of a mouse that lived in trees.

From this tree mouse all mammals, from horses to history teachers descended. So, not only *did* humanity not live at the same time as the dinosaurs, humanity *could not* have lived at the same time as the dinosaurs.

All the same ... in 1960, H. L. Armstrong published a

MEXICAN MYSTERY

paper in the prestigious scientific journal *Nature* dealing with fossil human footprints found near the Paluxy River, in Texas. Dinosaur footprints were found in the same strata. In 1983, the *Moscow News* reported the discovery of a fossilised human footprint next to the fossil footprint of a three-toed dinosaur in the Turkmen Republic.

In 1968, a fossil collector named William J. Meister split open a block of shale in Utah, and found a fossilised human shoe print. There were trilobite fossils in the same stone. Trilobites are even older than the dinosaurs.

Your teachers will tell you all the footprints mentioned are fakes, not as old as they look, or genuine fossils created by some hitherto unknown dinosaur that just happened to walk on two legs and have feet identical to those of modern humans.

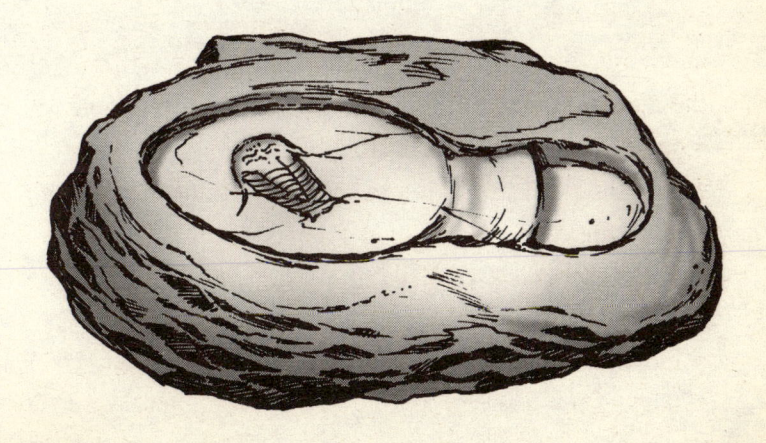

ATLANTIS

But the notion that humans have been around far longer than modern scientists believe doesn't just rely on the evidence of fossil footprints. According to a report in *The Geologist* a human skeleton was found 30 metres below the surface in a coal seam at Macoupin County, Ilinois. The seam in which it was found dated between 286 and 320 million years BC.

Chapter 31
MEMORIES OF ATLANTIS

Despite everything your textbooks say, there seems to be very little doubt that at least one advanced civilisation existed in the dark depths of prehistory. But was that civilisation Atlantis? Even if you forget about Plato, there's still rather a lot of evidence for Atlantis if you take the trouble to look for it. All of it points in the same direction, making a case that's hard to ignore.

Take, for example, the fact that the Atlantic Ocean used to be called the *Mare Tenebrosum*, the gloomy sea, and was referred to in Greek records as muddy, shallow, dark and misty. You have to ask yourself why. Today, the Atlantic is neither shallow, muddy nor dark, but if it matched that description in classical times, then we have support for Plato's claim that the destruction of Atlantis filled the sea with mud and interfered with navigation.

There are also echoes of Atlantis throughout world mythology. This is particularly true of the ten kings of Atlantis Plato mentioned. Norse mythology mentions ten ancestors of Odin, the chief of the gods. Arabian histories recall ten 'Kings of the Adites' who lived long ago. In China, the most ancient records speak of ten emperors who ruled in prehistoric times.

The sacred texts of India, a curious mixture of history and religion, list nine Brahmadikas and their founder, Brahma, who together make up the Ten Fathers of civilisation. The legends of Iran claim that the oldest Iranian civilisation began with the reign of ten 'Peisdadien Kings' described as 'men of the ancient law.'

Clay tablets found in the ruins of Sumeria, the earliest civilisation in the world according to your textbooks, tell of an even earlier culture that lasted for thousands of years and was ruled by ... ten kings.

There are even more direct references scattered throughout history. In Greek myth, King Midas of Phrygia, a man so rich his very touch was believed to turn things to gold, received a report of a great Atlantic continent 'larger than Asia, Europe and Libya put together' whose inhabitants built enormous cities.

The Roman historian Timagenes recorded in the 1st Century BC that certain tribes of Gaul (modern France) were descended from Atlantean invaders. Marcellus, a more widely read Roman historian, wrote of seven

MEMORIES OF ATLANTIS

Atlantic islands whose inhabitants preserved memories of Atlantis as a greater island which had for a long time dominated the smaller ones.

If you accept history as described by modern textbooks, the Americas – North and South – were isolated from the rest of the world until the late 15th Century. Plato's Atlantis account suggests they were nothing of the sort – the Atlanteans established colonies in South America which then had links with the rest of the world.

We know what tends to happen when people from one area move to colonise another: they often name their new home in memory of their old one. You can see the process illustrated on any modern atlas. New York is named after York in England (and was once named after Amsterdam in Holland). There is a Paris in Texas, named after the capital of France. New South Wales is an Australian state. New France is part of Canada.

If the Atlanteans colonised their world, we might expect to find something similar happening. Since we no longer know the names of Atlantean cities we can't make a direct comparison. But we can keep a look-out for ancient cities in the Old World which are identical to, or at least closely resemble, long established place names in the New World.

You could do worse than start your search in the works of Ptolemy, an Egyptian geographer who lived in the 2nd Century AD. He lists no fewer than five ancient

ATLANTIS

cities of Armenia that have counterparts in Central America. The cities are Chol, Colua, Zuivana, Cholima and Zalissa. The Central American locations are Chol-ula, Colua-can, Zuivan, Colima and Xalisco (pronounced Zalisso.) Perhaps the most impressive memory of Atlantis is a tradition preserved by the Aztecs of South America.

Historically speaking, the Aztecs were a relatively recent people. They ruled a large empire in what is now central and southern Mexico during the 15th and early 16th Centuries. They were also extraordinarily sophisticated. Their capital, Tenochtitlan, was literally built in the middle of a lake. They began work on the city in 1325 by excavating mud from the Lake of the Moon to make a series of artificial islands which they then turned into kitchen gardens. Then they built the city itself on a central island connected to the mainland by a series of causeways and bridges.

Tenochtitlan was, to say the least, impressive. It had more than 500 stone-built palaces, each one crowned with battlements and decorated with serpents. It had 40 huge mansions for the nobility and thousands of solidly constructed buildings, laid out in a logical grid, for the remaining population. Dominating the whole was a grouping of limestone-faced pyramids topped by monumental temples.

Aqueducts were installed to bring in fresh, clean water. A series of interlinked canals provided a hugely

MEMORIES OF ATLANTIS

Tenochtitlan

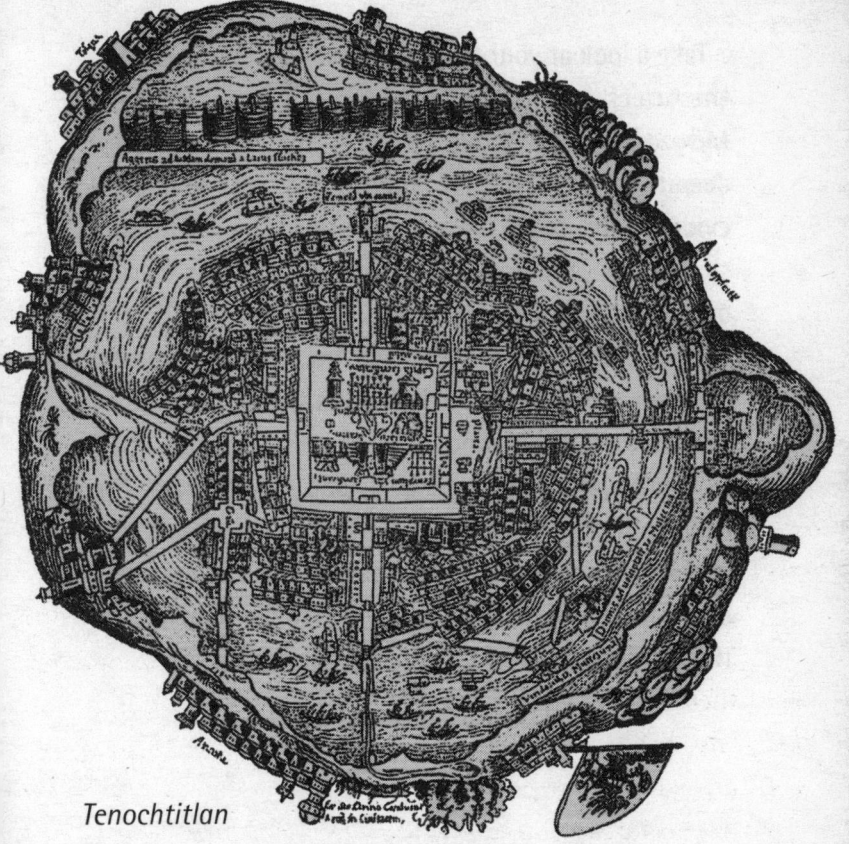

efficient public transportation system, similar to the Italian city of Venice today. The whole place covered 7.5 square kilometres and housed 300,000 citizens. The Aztecs were a warlike people and steadily expanded an empire – linked by well-made paved roads – throughout central and southern Mexico until they were stopped by even more bloodthirsty invaders, the Spanish conquistadors in 1519.

ATLANTIS

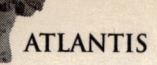

Take a look at your textbooks and you'll discover that the Aztecs were supposed to have come from northern Mexico (and emigrated south in the 14th Century) despite the fact that there's no archaeological evidence of their having developed there. In fact there's no archaeological evidence of their having developed anywhere in South America. It's as if their ancestors suddenly arrived there from somewhere else.

Which is exactly what the Aztecs themselves had to say about it. According to their own histories, their race originated long ago in a land 'to the east'. The nearest land to the east of South America is the African continent. But the Aztecs didn't say that they came from Africa. They said they came from a land that no longer existed. They called it Aztlan.

Chapter 32

LOST LEMURIA

Despite the evidence, Atlantis has never been popular with scientists. But in the 19th Century, they did rather take to the idea of another lost continent, located somewhere in the Indian or Pacific Oceans, which they decided to call Lemuria.

What gave them the idea of this continent was that animal and plant life was – or had been – remarkably similar on two sides of the Indian Ocean. Out of 35 fossil species found in Natal (South Africa) for example, 22 were exactly the same as those found in southern India. Rock structures were very close as well.

A zoologist named P. L. Sclater came up with the theory that if animals and plants of two countries were alike, then there had to be a geographical connnection, past or present, between them. In other words, there had to be an easy way for the plants and animals to spread from one territory to the other.

ATLANTIS

Since thousands of kilometres of open ocean isn't easy by any definition, Dr Sclater reckoned there must once have been an extensive landmass in between. He decided to call it after the lemur, a sweet little monkey-like creature with a nice tail now found only in Madagascar and neighbouring islands, but once thought to inhabit most of the northern hemisphere.

Lemuria, Dr Sclater thought, might once have stretched from the Malay Archipelago across the south coast of Asia to Madagascar, an island off the south eastern coast of Africa.

Dr Sclater was a well respected Fellow of the Royal Society and his ideas caught on. Distinguished scientists like Thomas Huxley and Alfred Russel Wallace thought the former existence of Lemuria was 'highly probable'. The German biologist Ernst Haeckel decided it was the cradle of the human race, a sort of Garden of Eden on which we evolved from anthropoid (man-like) apes.

To the scientists' dismay, the theory of Lemuria was promptly taken up by an extraordinary woman named Helena Petrovna Blavatsky. As you could probably guess by the name, Madame Blavatsky was Russian by birth, but she sailed into Britain in Victorian times claiming loudly that 'Secret Masters' living in Tibet and other far-off places had taught her the hidden history of the human race.

According to this history, five root races – all now

long gone – had come before modern humanity. The first lived on a mysterious continent known as 'the Imperishable Sacred Land' and associated by some with Antarctica, the second in a 'Hyperborean Continent' off the north of Asia, the third in Lemuria, the fourth in Atlantis and the fifth in America. (The sixth race, to which we all belong, is apparently evolving into a seventh of super beings.)

Madame Blavatsky located Lemuria in the Pacific rather than the Indian Ocean, claiming that the South Sea Islands were all that remained of it today. So great was her influence that the Indian Ocean Lemuria was quietly forgotten and the idea of a lost Pacific continent was firmly implanted in the public mind.

Pacific Visits

While other Central and South American peoples maintained, like the Aztecs, that their distant ancestors came across the Atlantic from the east, the ancient Central American Mayan people wrote about at least one visit from the other direction, across the Pacific, when a great leader called Tutul Xiu voyaged from a land called Tulupan. Incredibly, there is some suggestion Tulupan may have been China – a Buddhist monk named Hwui Shan described an ancient expedition to Mexico led by a Chinese nobleman named Tui-lu. Other texts tell of successful Chinese and Japanese voyages across the Pacific dating as far back as 3000 BC.

ATLANTIS

It was an idea that was to surface again in the 20th Century – with a name change from Lemuria to Mu – aided by the work of someone we've already met in this book, the Scots archaeologist William Niven who found that 50,000-year-old buried city in Mexico.

You'll recall that among Niven's discoveries were more than 2,600 ancient tablets inscribed with what appeared to be pictographic writing. These were all smooth water-worn stones carved with curious symbols – and sometimes human figures. Understandably excited by his find, Niven showed the tablets to various experts both in America and overseas, but nobody was able to offer a translation. Indeed, nobody had ever seen anything like them before.

With no help forthcoming from his fellow archaeologists, Niven made tracings of the tablets and sent them to an old friend of his named James Churchward. Churchward wasn't an archaeologist but an adventurer. During his lifetime he was variously a colonel in the Indian Army, a tea planter, a civil engineer, an inventor, a steel magnate and a world traveller. Astonishingly, he recognised the pictographic script at once.

Churchward claimed that while he was living in India, he became friendly with a Hindu priest while they were both engaged in famine relief work. The priest taught him an ancient language called Naacal,

LOST LEMURIA

believed to be the original tongue of mankind.

Knowledge of this language later helped Churchward translate a set of stone tablets, held for safekeeping in a Tibetan monastery, which contained 'sacred inspired writings' originating on the lost continent of Mu.

Mu, like Blavatsky's Lemuria, was a vast land in the Pacific Ocean centred a little south of the equator and measuring some 5,000 kilometres (about 3,000 miles) from north to south, 10,000 kilometres (about 6,000

miles) from east to west. It stretched literally from Hawaii to Fiji and was divided into three major landmasses separated by narrow stretches of water. Although it perished at much the same time as Plato's Atlantis, tiny remnants survive to this day in the form of Pacific islands bearing the ruins of gigantic megalithic statues and buildings.

Churchward told his friend Niven that the pictographs of the Mexican tablets were a form of Naacal and the story they told confirmed – and indeed enlarged – the Tibetan account of Mu. And what an account it was.

Mu was very, very old – just as old as Atlantis, in fact. (And Churchward claimed he'd seen a map in Tibet showing Atlantis joined to Europe, Africa and America during a time when huge creatures roamed the world and 'monstrous forms' filled the seas.)

The Pacific continent was a tropical, fertile environment so expertly farmed that it was able to support a population of 64,000,000. These were the people who established the world's first civilisation, then exported their culture as they colonised vast swathes of the planet.

Various races lived peacefully under the banner of a single government and built huge palaces and temples. Like Hapgood's ancient sea kings, their ships sailed the oceans of the world, leaving signs of their progress as far apart as the Middle East and Asia.

At its height, Mu had colonised most of the Americas. It founded a culture that stretched from the west coast of North America to the east coast of South America as far as modern-day Argentina. It engineered a vast central American canal, linking east and west coasts with an inland Amazon Sea (now long dried up) and allowing Atlantic access to the continent of Atlantis with which it had strong trade links.

Many former Mu colonies became independent and established empires of their own. The most impressive of these was the Uighur Empire, which stretched across the whole of Asia and Europe as far as the British Isles. Its ancient capital now lies buried 15 metres beneath the sands of the Gobi Desert.

But there were other important colonies as well. Egypt, India and Burma were all colonised by Mu – indeed the civilisations of the Babylonians, Chaldeans, Egyptians, Greeks, Hindus and Persians all derived, directly or indirectly from the great Pacific culture.

Mu was also indirectly responsible for two of the world's great religions, Judaism and Christianity. A man named Osiris, born in Atlantis around 20000 BC, became tired with the faith of his home country, which had fallen into superstition and corruption. He travelled to Mu for spiritual guidance and there became a great mystic master.

When he returned to Atlantis, Osiris established a new (or possibly revised) religion of simplicity, love and peace, installing himself as High Priest in the process. Another man named Thoth carried this religion to Egypt some 4,000 years later. (Both Osiris and Thoth are now listed among the gods of Ancient Egypt.)

Transplanted into Egypt, the ideas of Mu became the foundation of Moses' concept of a single God, while the doctrines of Jesus were, according to Churchward, word for word those of the original Osiris.

Chapter 33
EVIDENCE FOR LEMURIA

Colonel Churchward's romantic picture of Mu sounds too good to be true; and the sad fact is that when something sounds too good to be true, that's usually just the way it really is.

To be honest, the Colonel wasn't the sort of man you'd really want to take on trust. He came from a good enough background and he had an excellent education at Oxford and Sandhurst. His military career wasn't particularly distinguished – he was in the Royal Engineers and the Lancers – but there was nothing much wrong with it either.

After his marriage broke up, he resigned his commission and became a tea planter. He liked to quote the proverb, 'Adventures turn up for Adventurers' and adventures certainly turned up for him. When he finally emigrated to the United States, he quickly developed a reputation as a teller of tall tales. He also had a talent for making enemies.

Colonel Churchward published four popular books on Mu between 1930 and 1934 and there have been those who suggested his motive was not so much an interest in ancient history as a desire to make up for some of the money he lost when a recent venture into the steel business collapsed.

Maybe more to the point, Churchward made a lot of claims about Mu, but backed them with very little evidence. As far as I know, he was the only scholar to see the Naacal Tablets he was given in Tibet. His books reproduced no photographs of them and even the illustrations he claimed to have drawn from them were few and far between.

Although he stated firmly that the tablets William Niven discovered were in Naacal too and supported his Tibetan sources, you have to take his word for this since nobody else, then or now, has been able to translate the Mexican finds.

Forbidden Facts About Carbon Dating

Scientists have a curious habit of presenting carbon dating as if it gave an absolutely definitive and accurate age for everything it tests. In fact, carbon dating techniques will only work on organic matter, so they're useless for ancient stone or fossils. They don't work at all on anything more than 40,000 years old,

EVIDENCE FOR LEMURIA

> *they produce results that are always 3% too young, are subject to contamination that can make final readings a nonsense and means some are more accurate than others. As if that wasn't enough, carbon dating animal tissue can be thrown out significantly by the diet of the animal.*

You might also be a little suspicious of the fact that several aspects of Churchward's story – the great age of humanity, the existence of a Pacific continent, the spiritual existence of ancient man before gradually solidifying into our current material form – were all part and parcel of Madame Blavatsky's doctrines, now part of her Theosophical Society and attracting considerable interest. Anyone who jumped on that bandwagon might make a name for himself ... and quite possibly a little cash.

Furthermore, Churchward claimed his Naacal Tablets contained Masonic symbols that showed the origins of Freemasonry went back perhaps 70,000 years ... thus echoing the work of his own brother, Dr Albert Churchward who was a writer on the relationship of Freemasonry with ancient mankind.

But while the story of Mu/Lemuria is suspicious to say the least, there is still some evidence to support it – or at least to support the existence, in comparitively recent times, of a now-lost Pacific continent. For example, the Russian geologist V. V. Belousov engaged in studies which led him to announce that 'very recently, partially even in the age of man, the Pacific Ocean grew considerably at the expense of great chunks of continents which, together with their young ranges of mountains, were inundated (flooded) by it.' Belousov added that the summits of these mountains were now the many little islands surrounding the countries of East Asia.

Belousov is not alone. A study of fossil trilobites led the French geologist R. Fuson to conclude that what is now the underwater Hawaiian Ridge was once above water and part of a very large landmass, making the Hawaiian islands no more than high ground in a Pacific continent. This continent existed until relatively recently and may have aided the spread of humanity from Asia westward to the Americas and southward to Polynesia.

Delegates to the Tenth World Pacific Congress were treated to a paper by America's George H. Cronwell reporting on the discovery of coal on the Pacific island of Rapaiti. Coal forms through the action of massive pressures on the remains of prehistoric forests, a process that can't occur in the isolated environment of a tiny island. Cronwell concluded that the evidence showed that a huge landmass had once existed south of Polynesia was now undeniable.

There is even evidence of an advanced culture, now long lost, in the region. Archaeologists excavating on

EVIDENCE FOR LEMURIA

islands in the Southwest Pacific, discovered more than 400 man-made cement cylinders 100–200 centimetres in diameter and up to 250 centimetres long. They were speckled with silica and iron gravel and were dated as 13,000 years old.

Prehistoric stone-built structures on the Pacific island of Ponape and several neighbouring islands indicate the presence in ancient times of yet another unknown civilisation. Records contain a report of ancient sea walls, vaults, enclosures and other vast masonry, some of it 6 metres high and over 3 metres thick.

Stone tower on Ponape

ATLANTIS

A group of more than 90 man-made islands surrounds Ponape covering an area of approximately 28 square kilometres (11 square miles). The group is protected by a reef, but to the east where the reef is broken, the ancient builders constructed a massive breakwater which stretches south for 5 kilometres (3 miles). The stone used in much of this work was transported a distance of almost 48 kilometres (30 miles). The artificial islands are raised on basalt platforms anywhere from 1.5 to over 3 metres above water level, then topped by huge walls – in one case 10 metres high and over 3 metres thick. The remains have been described as 'among the world's prehistoric wonders'.

They are wonders that are likely to remain uninvestigated for some time, since the area is now home to United States naval and air force bases. But the evidence, from various sources examined in the last two chapters, suggests there was not just one lost continent, but two.

A populated landmass seems to have existed in the Pacific at much the same time as Atlantis ... and disappeared just as completely.

Chapter 34

THE DEATH OF ATLANTIS

So what happened? According to Plato, all of Atlantis – and much of Athens – sank in a single day and a night. Is it really possible for this to happen to an entire continent?

Well, it's happening to Australia as we speak. As that great Pacific continent drifts north towards Asia, its leading edge has tilted and gone down by a massive 200 metres.

But the process has taken 100 million years so far, too slow to explain what may have happened to Atlantis. Plato claimed that the Atlantis sinking came at a time of great earthquakes. Was this, perhaps, the reason why it sank?

Believe it or not, there are 50,000 earthquakes somewhere in the world every year – almost 1,000 a week. You don't hear much about them because all but about 100 are too small to cause much trouble. (A few years ago I lived through an earthquake in Ireland without even noticing.) But among that remaining 100 there have been a few that made considerable – and often tragic – impact.

In 1775, a quake centred on Lisbon in Portugal caused damage in Algiers, more than 1,000 kilometres away, and sent out a tidal wave that hit Martinique, 6,100 kilometres away.

In 1964, huge tracts of land rose and fell as the result of an Alaskan earthquake. The effects were felt over an area of 1,300,000 square kilometres. A region of 120,000 square kilometres was tilted violently, hills were thrust as high as 25 metres, while other areas of land sank to a depth of 2.5 metres. There were vast landslides and a tidal wave so enormous that it caused damage in distant California. The main quake was followed by *tens of thousands* of aftershocks.

It was possibly the most devastating event of the entire 20th Century ... but it came nowhere close to sinking North America. In fact, since the death toll was so small – only 131 people – it hardly rated a mention in the newspapers.

Plato also mentioned floods. The association with earthquakes is interesting because if you get an undersea (or even coastal) quake greater than 6.5 on the Richter Scale, it's likely to cause what the Japanese call a *tsunami*, or tidal wave.

In deep water, a tsunami is nothing. On a ship at sea, you wouldn't even notice its passing. But when it reaches shallow water, it's a very different story. The wave can grow to a height of 35 metres or more and travel thousands of kilometres before crashing down on a coastline at speeds of up to 720 kilometres an hour.

As you might imagine, this sort of occurrence can be disastrous for port cities – which, if you consult your atlas, you'll find to be just about every major city in the world. In the late 1900s, a single tsunami killed 36,000 people in the East Indies. The 2005 tsunami in the Indian Ocean also had a death toll measured in the tens of thousands. All the same, there has never been so much as a hint of a tsunami large enough to drown a single country, let alone a continent. You may be in danger of your life if you live on the coast, but move some kilometres inland and you're safe as houses. Since the mathematics of a tsunami are now well known – the eventual height of the wave depends of the intensity of the original quake, the distance travelled across an ocean and the depth of the coastal waters – you can confidently predict that bad as they are, these great waves won't get any worse.

Apart from tsunami, flooding tends to occur as the result of heavy rainfall over a brief period of time. Simple though it sounds, this can cause considerable damage, as the authorities of most major cities can tell you. Paris was hit by catastrophic floods in 1658 and 1910, as was Warsaw in 1861 and 1964, Frankfurt in 1854 and 1930 and Rome in 1530 and 1557.

Anywhere on or near a river is potentially subject to periodic flooding. Before the building of the Aswan Dam, the annual Nile floods were a feature of life in Egypt. These were caused by seasonal rains far to the south in the highlands of Ethiopia, but rainfall isn't always the reason for river flooding. In colder climates, ice jams associated with the spring rise can cause enormous problems, as has happened at least four times with the Danube and once in the 19th Century with the Neva in Russia.

Storm tides can cause severe flooding as well. It's happened fairly frequently in the Netherlands, it's happened in Belgium and it happened along the English coast in 1953.

But for all the heartbreak and damage flooding can cause, even a deluge as experienced by Noah in the Bible – forty days and forty nights of constant heavy rain – would not be enough to drown an entire continent.

If not earthquakes or simple floods, is there any other natural phenomenon that might have caused Atlantis to disappear? On the face of it, the most likely candidate is volcanic action. Only a few years ago, there were excited television reports of a brand new

THE DEATH OF ATLANTIS

landmass – a volcanic island that had appeared virtually overnight off the coast of Iceland.

The story didn't last. After a few rumbling weeks, the island sank back into the troubled seabed from which it had erupted. But if it could happen on this scale, could it also happen to a country 'the size of Libya and Asia (Minor)'? If Atlantis straddled a fracture in the Earth's crust like the San Andreas Fault, could volcanic action have destroyed it overnight?

There's one well-known historical parallel for the sudden disappearance if not of a civilisation, at least of a city – or rather two cities more or less simultaneously.

The thriving Roman cities of Pompeii and Herculaneum were destroyed together with several smaller communities, by the eruption of Mount Vesuvius in AD 79. Pompeii supported between 10,000 and 20,000 inhabitants at the time of its destruction.

Archaeological detective work, supported by an eyewitness account from the Roman philosopher Pliny, have given us a vivid picture of what happened on the fateful day.

Just after midday on August 24, fragments of ash, pumice and other volcanic debris began pouring down on Pompeii, quickly covering the city to a depth of more than 3 metres and causing the roofs of many houses to fall in. Surges of volcanic material and heated gas reached the city walls on the morning of

August 25 and soon choked to death those residents who had not been killed by falling debris.

Additional lava flows and rains of ash followed, adding at least another 3 metres of debris and preserving the bodies of the inhabitants who perished while taking shelter in their houses or trying to escape toward the coast. The city remained buried under a layer of pumice stones and ash 6 to 7 metres deep.

The particular circumstances of Herculaneum led to burial of that city beneath a compact mass of material about 15 to 18 metres deep. Unlike Pompeii, few bodies were found in the city itself, but more than 100 were buried while fleeing on the roads outside. But devastating though this was to the citizens of the

THE DEATH OF ATLANTIS

cities, it made not one whit of difference to Roman culture as a whole. Roman civilisation flourished, the Roman Empire continued to expand.

At one time, experts decided there really was a volcanic eruption that destroyed an entire early civilisation. It occurred on the Aegean island of Thera sometime around 1500 BC and, so the theory went, caused the downfall of the great seafaring Minoan civilisation centred on the island of Crete some 110 kilometres (70 miles) to the south.

You can see how the theory came about. The Thera eruption was up there among the very largest ever recorded. Vast quantities of ash and pumice were thrown into the upper atmosphere and carried by the prevailing winds as far as the Middle East. There has been speculation that the Biblical plagues of Egypt, which caused the pharaoh to allow Moses to lead the Jews out of bondage, were actually the result of the Thera explosion.

In 1939, a Greek archaeologist named Spyridon Marinatos went a step further to suggest the eruption led to the collapse of the Minoan civilization. He put forward the vision of fire raining from the skies to destroy Minoan buildings and ash wiping out the Cretan harvests.

Since the Minoan civilisation really did collapse around this time, it was a tempting explanation and several academics built on the Marinatos theory to claim that here was the source of the Atlantis legend – a great civilisation destroyed over a matter of days during a disastrous time of earthquake and flood. Plato just got his timing wrong, that was all.

But alas for these claims, evidence gathered in the 1980s showed that the Minoan civilisation survived long after the Thera eruption and the amount of debris and ash that fell on Crete was not enough to destroy crops or even cause significant damage to property.

Besides which, Thera still exists, now called Santorini. It's only half as big as it once was, but remains a flourishing, populated island that grows grapes for wine and exports pumice (hardened lava). The huge eruption failed to sink it.

The most famous volcanic eruption of all time caused worldwide effects, but, like Thera, failed to sink very much in the way of a landmass. Krakatoa, an Indonesian island between Sumatra and Java, blew on August 26, 1883, with a bang that was heard 4,800 kilometres away in Australia. An 80-kilometre-high cloud of ash caused worldwide harvest failures in the following months and produced spectacular sunsets everywhere for several years. The tidal wave it caused killed 36,000 people. But for all the violence, only 23 square kilometres of Krakatoa island disappeared beneath the sea. The rest still stands to this day.

There's a worrying super-volcano in the United States, just under Yellowstone National Park. The last

THE DEATH OF ATLANTIS

time it blew, about 2 milion years ago, it spewed ash over 19 western states and parts of Canada and Mexico – enough of it to bury New York State to a depth of 20 metres. There are indications it may be about to blow again some day soon. If it does, it will be a horrific catastrophe, but it will not sink America beneath the Atlantic Ocean. We know this because the Yellowstone super-volcano has blown more than 100 times before without damaging the structure of the continent.

There's an area in India called the Deccan Traps that shows signs of ancient volcanic activity so violent, so extreme, that some scientists think this, rather than a massive meteor impact, was what caused the death of the dinosaurs. It was arguably the largest volcanic explosion in the history of our planet, covering an area of 500,000 square kilometres. But India is still here.

From all the evidence, it seems volcanic activity can never get up enough steam to sink an entire continent or anything remotely like it.

So what was it that really destroyed Atlantis?

Chapter 35

THE SHIFTING EARTH

There's a mystery in the North. Fossil remains of magnolia and fig have been discovered in Greenland. These plants require not only heat but light. Northern Greenland has a six-month Arctic night. There is absolutely no way magnolia and fig could grow there now.

There are coal seams in the Spitsbergen Archipelago. Coal is the end result of geological pressures on ancient forests and other vegetation. This turns them first into peat bogs, then into coal seams. In Spitsbergen, the ancient forests were growing only 8° 15' from the North Pole. This sort of forestation is quite impossible today. Coral growths have been found around Canada, Greenland and Alaska. Coral can only form in the tropics. Yet, impossibly, it formed at one time in these chill polar seas.

THE SHIFTING EARTH

The mammoth is a huge elephant-like creature that became extinct around 8000 BC. We know quite a lot about it because several mammoth carcasses have been found perfectly preserved in the permafrost of Siberia. But these finds represent just the tip of a mammoth iceberg. There were so many of the creatures in Siberia that fossil ivory has been a major export to China and Europe since medieval times.

Mammoths were giant vegetarians. Today, an African elephant eats about a tonne of vegetation every week. Mammoths needed even more. What grows in frozen Siberia now would scarcely support a single member of the species, let alone the vast herds that once lived there. From all this, it's clear that our northlands were once a lot less cold. In fact, the evidence is that certain areas must have been positively tropical. At some time in the past the climate changed.

But it didn't change gradually. Some of those preserved mammoths died standing up, uninjured, with buttercups and grasses in their mouths and undigested plants in their stomach. There is only one process that could cause a death like that. They were flash frozen where they stood.

In 1953, Professor Hapgood – the same Professor Hapgood who studied ancient maps – put forward a solution to these mysteries when he published a book on what he called the theory of global crust displacement.

This theory suggested that there were widely separated periods during which the entire crust of Planet Earth moved significantly. Such shifts, possibly caused by an irregular build-up of ice at the pole, meant previously temperate or tropical regions were carried into the Arctic or Antarctic circles, causing an abrupt plunge in temperatures and wiping out whole categories of warm-weather plants and animals.

At the same time as temperate regions moved into the cold, frozen areas were shifted into the warm. As a result, vast quantities of ice quickly melted, causing a dramatic rise in sea levels throughout the globe.

THE SHIFTING EARTH

According to Hapgood, crustal displacement was neither gradual nor smooth. It was accompanied by violent earthquakes and gigantic tidal waves, causing mass destruction and mass extinctions. The last period of crustal displacement, he suspected, marked the extinction of the mammoths ... and explained those buttercups.

Shortly before he died, Professor Hapgood wrote to a colleague about the work he was doing on a new, updated edition of *Earth's Shifting Crust*, the book in which he put forward his theory. He had, he said, found evidence that the last crustal displacement had moved both American continents south by some 3,200 kilometres (2,000 miles), devastating every living thing on them.

Interestingly, there is sound geological evidence that the North Pole is not where it used to be. It has, in fact, occupied several different locations at different time periods. There is also sound geological evidence of another curious phenomenon which may or may not be connected.

The Earth, as you probably know, is a giant magnet with its northern, positive pole, close to, but not identical with, the geographical North Pole – hence mariners can use a magnetic compass to find out what direction they happen to be sailing. Most people assume that the magnetic pole (as it's known) has always been much the same as it is today, but this is not the case. The magnetic alignment of iron particles in various rock strata indicates that the magnetic poles, north and south, have abruptly reversed themselves on several occasions throughout prehistory.

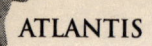

Nobody knows what caused these reversals or how much, if any, damage was caused to the world in the process. But if magnetic changes were linked to Hapgood's crustal displacement and continents the size of the Americas can move thousands of kilometres in a brief space of time, then suddenly we have a mechanism that really could explain the disappearance of Atlantis. But it's not the only explanation.

Chapter 36

THE FALLING SKY

Something dreadful happened in Siberia on the morning of June 30, 1908. Foresters in this remote area of Russia watched in awe as a fiery mass passed overhead. Then, at 7.40 a.m. came the explosion.

It was, in a word, gigantic – current estimates put it in the H-bomb range, equivalent to 10 or 15 megatonnes of TNT. In moments it had flattened a massive 2 million hectares of pine forest. The ground trembled, buildings shook and a hot wind threw people off their feet 80 kilometres (50 miles) away. The explosion itself was clearly visible at a distance of 800 kilometres (500 miles). So much vaporised material and gas was thrown into the atmosphere that there were abnormally bright night-time skies over the whole of Europe for weeks afterwards.

Something collided with the Earth that morning.

ATLANTIS

Scientists are unsure whether it was a giant asteroid or part of a comet. But they are fairly sure it struck at a speed of 100,000 km/h (62,000 mph) and weighed somewhere in the region of a million tonnes. Were it not for the isolation of the point of impact, the devastation and loss of life would have been enormous.

Things hit our planet all the time – some 15 objects every hour according to best estimates, rising to 75 an hour on a bad day. Most of them are so small they burn up in the atmosphere with scarcely a flicker. But some are big enough to make a show.

In the summer of 1972, something streaked across the daytime skies of Montana, Wyoming and Utah in the United States, moving at a speed of 53,900 km/h (33,500 mph). Satellite photos later showed it was a rock nearly 30 metres in diameter.

It was the brightest meteor ever recorded, but not the biggest. In 1920, they discovered one in Namibia that weighed more than 60 tonnes. But meteors are the least of our problems. Even bigger things have landed and bigger things are on their way.

Astronomers worry most about two things. The first is comets. Since records began (which is actually a long time ago as the Chinese have been watching the skies – and writing down their observations – for 2,200 years) over 800 comets have entered our solar system, many of them more than once. If even one of them had happened to collide with the Earth, the results would have been catastrophic – so catastrophic that you might well not be reading this now. (Comets – or at least bits of them – have struck the Earth in the very distant past. There's a chain of prehistoric impact craters in Chad, Central Africa, that scientists are fairly certain was caused by comet fragments. The craters are up to 10 miles in diameter and were caused by something close on 1.5 kilometres (1 mile) across.

The second thing astronomers worry about is asteroids. Asteroids are small planetary bodies of varying size. The largest, 1,030 kilometres (640 miles) in diameter, has been named Ceres. The smallest ... well, nobody really knows since it's probably too small to be detected by current telescopes.

You'll find most of the solar system's asteroids – and there are tens of thousands of them – in an enormous belt orbiting the sun between Mars and Jupiter. But some of them haven't stayed there. In 1932, a German astronomer spotted one that crossed the orbit of the Earth. This disturbing discovery started a search and today astronomers confidently estimate there are close on 2,000 asteroids almost a kilometre (half a mile) in diameter that regularly cross the orbit of our planet. The worry is there'll come a day that one of them will hit us.

If that day comes, disastrous though it will undoubtedly be, all the calculations show it will not sink a continent. In fact, most scientists can't even imagine what sort of disaster would sink a continent the way Plato described. But two exceptions are D. S. Allan and J. B. Delair, a couple of British academics who have put forward a theory that explains a lot of ancient mysteries and shows how Atlantis could have disappeared forever.

A very odd story appears in Jewish ancient legends. It describes how, in the distant past, the waters of the world piled up in a towering wall 2,570 kilometres (1,600 miles) high that could be seen 'by all the nations of the Earth'.

Could such a thing really have happened? It seems even more unlikely than the sinking of a continent, yet these two apparent myths may well be interlinked. According to the Allan/Delair theory, both may have resulted from a close pass to the Earth by a massive fragment of a supernova (exploding star). As it happens, there's a supernova that fits the timing. It was the Vela supernova that exploded a little more than 11,000 years ago. The results of the explosion could have reached our solar system in a few hundred years.

THE FALLING SKY

Today, anything thrown off by the Vela supernova is long gone, although a pulsating star remains in the sky to show where it all happened. But about the time Plato pinpointed as the sinking of Atlantis, we might imagine a huge fireball, bigger by far than our planet, hurtling past the orbits of Jupiter and Mars on a close approach to Earth.

Our distant ancestors saw it coming, a fire in the sky that must have looked like a miniature sun. In all likelihood they thought it was a god, since early myths frequently record a 'war of the gods' in the heavens. But this new god's real threat was to our home world.

Various forces are involved when one large astronomical body approaches too close to another. There is a gravitational effect, an electro magnetic exchange and, in the case of a burning supernova fragment, a heat exchange.

The resulting combination must have been utterly devastating. Since the Vela fragment was so much larger than our planet, it jerked the Earth out of orbit, caused its axis to tilt, slowed the speed of rotation and created a wobble that can still be measured by astronomers to this day.

The outer shell of our world began literally to crack. That too can be seen to this day in what's now called the Great Rift Valley which extends more than 4,800 kilometres (3,000 miles) from Syria in the Middle East to Mozambique in Africa and in parts is fully 160 kilometres (100 miles) wide.

Beneath the shell of the Earth, vast reservoirs of molten magma were drawn towards the intruder like a high tide in a fiery sea. Volcanoes erupted with horrific violence. Millions of tonnes of hot ash were hurled into the atmosphere. Lava oozed from hundreds of thousands of new fissures. Mountain ranges thrust up. Earthquakes rumbled continuously.

As the supernova fragment came even closer, its radiation began to raise the temperature of our entire world. The change in planetary rotation triggered global tornadoes that flattened whole forests and whipped tonnes more dust and debris into the atmosphere. A dreadful darkness spread across the face of the Earth.

In days, the entire world was transformed into a screaming chaos of tempest, darkness, heat, earthquake and flood. Stone buildings collapsed like matchsticks. Fresh water was polluted and supplies

THE FALLING SKY

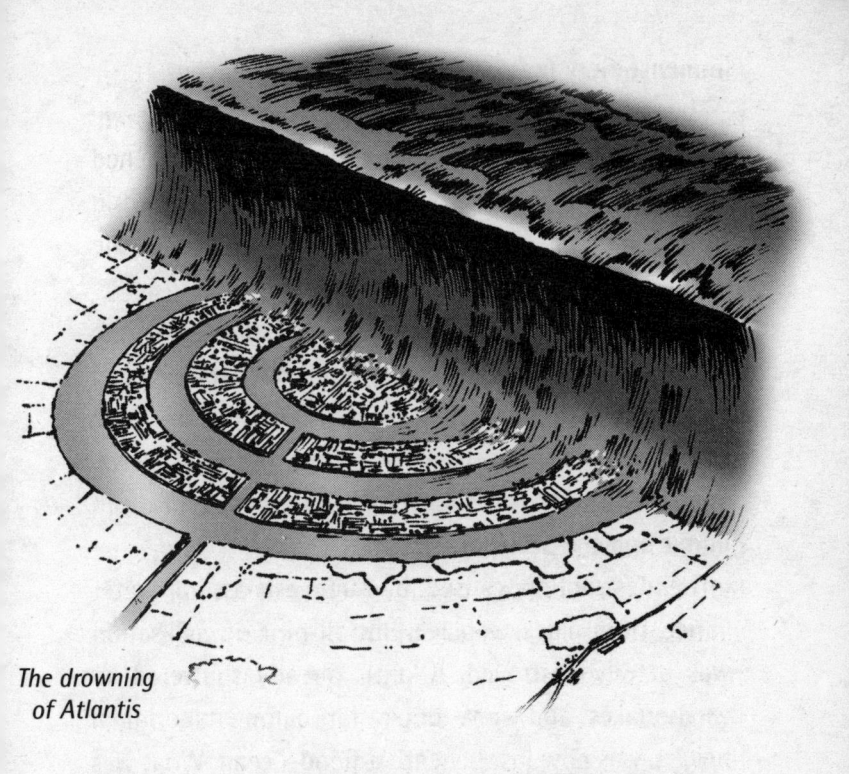

The drowning of Atlantis

dried up. The ground swelled and buckled. Choking volcanic gas was released. There was noise everywhere, day and night. Vast tracts of land simply sank. Among them was the entire continent of Atlantis.

As the intruder hurtled past, its massive gravity began to grip the world's oceans. Nearly 71% of the Earth's surface is covered by water to an average depth of 3,800 metres. This vast body of liquid was drawn northwards in a nightmare tide. As the gravitational attraction peaked, the waters of the world began to pile up in a gigantic standing wave, sucked towards the immense fiery mass that now filled the heavens.

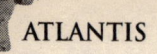

Then, as the Vela fragment began, at last, to move away from the Earth, the gravitational pull weakened and the standing wave broke. The water of the world rushed south in a raging torrent remembered in the flood legends of every ancient culture.

It was this surging wall of water that lifted the erratics. A gigantic flood that did not have the physical problems of glaciers in climbing hills or even mountains – it simply broke over them in a giant wave, depositing debris on their northern aspect and often mimicking the scour of ice.

The destruction caused by such a mass of water varied from place to place. But all hint of civilisation was utterly destroyed. Atlantis already shattered by earthquakes and sunk down far below its original height, was now lost beneath a flood-ocean. What was left of humanity took refuge where it could.

As the floodwaters drained to form new seas and oceans in the freshly created basins of a tortured Earth, humanity emerged from its worst nightmare into a broken, desolate world.

Chapter 37
THE AFTERMATH

Interestingly, the ideas put forward by Allan and Delair solve all the problems raised by Ice Age theory. First, you have the abrupt rise in temperature needed to trigger an Ice Age. The resulting increase in atmospheric moisture would collect around the volcanic dust to create a global downfall like Noah's flood. In the north, the flood would fall as snow and, once the standing wave broke, the remnants would quickly freeze to create a brand-new polar ice cap.

Constant rain worldwide would quickly bring down global temperatures ... and keep them down for years. The appearance of high mountain ranges (created by the earlier volcanic activity) added the final factor. They acted as glacier generators. Once you stop trying to explain what were really the effects of deluge and

ATLANTIS

flood, you can imagine glacial movement that no longer contradicts the laws of physics. You can imagine a belated Ice Age without the enormous sea of ice that lay at the heart of the original theory. The Ice Age that actually seized our world was far more short-lived than modern science credits. It began to lose its grip perhaps as early as 8000 BC and the last of its effects disappeared in a period of general global warming some 2,000 years later.

Humanity, devastated by the catastrophe, fought to survive and quickly forgot its civilised roots. Culture returned to the Stone Age and only slowly emerged from the hunter-gatherer stage to rediscover the arts of farming and begin again to build cities.

The Vela theory also explains something else – our shattered solar system. For the supernova fragment did a lot more than devastate the prehistoric civilisations of Earth. It shifted planetary orbits, broke up moons and may possibly have caused one planet to explode.

And in the process, it drowned a legend – one of the most intriguing civilisations our world has ever known: the fabled lost continent of Atlantis.

Further reading

The works that follow are just a few that were useful to me in writing the present book. They'll be just as useful to you if you want to take your studies of Atlantis further.

All of them are worth reading, but if time is short, you might like to concentrate mainly on…

- ***When the Earth Nearly Died***, which like most academic books is fairly heavy going, but gives you a wealth of hard evidence on the Vela supernova theory and pinpoints the problems with the sort of Ice Age theory you've been taught at school.
- ***The Atlantis Blueprint***, which is a good introduction to Professor Hapgood's shifting crust theory and presents intriguing new evidence for both crustal movement and the existence of an advanced prehistoric civilisation.
- And my own ***The Atlantis Enigma***, which enlarges on the material in the current book and presents far more detailed evidence to support most aspects of the subject presented here.

But here's the full list. Armed with name, author and publisher, your local bookshop should be able to order any that they don't already have in stock.

Ancient Inventions by Peter James and Nick Thorpe, Ballantine Books, New York, 1994.

Ancient Man: A Handbook of Puzzling Artifacts by William R. Corliss. The Sourcebook Project, Glen Arm, MD, 1980.

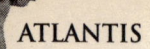

Forbidden Archaeology, the Hidden History of the Human Race by Michael A. Cremo and Richard L. Thompson. The Bhaktivedanta Institute, San Diego, 1993.

Maps of the Ancient Sea Kings, by Charles H. Hapgood. Adventures Unlimited Press, Illinois, 1996.

Martian Genesis, by Herbie Brennan. Piatkus Books, London, 1998.

Mysteries of the Mexican Pyramids by Peter Tompkins. Thames & Hudson, London, 1987.

Plato Prehistorian: 10,000, to 5,000 BC. Myth, Religion, Archaeology by Mary Settegast. Lindisfarne Press, New York, 1990.

The Atlantis Blueprint by Rand Flem-Ath and Colin Wilson. Little, Brown, London, 2000.

The Atlantis Enigma by Herbie Brennan. Piatkus Books, London, 1999.

The Earth's Shifting Crust: A Key to Some Basic Problems of Earth Science, by Charles H. Hapgood. Pantheon Books, New York, 1958.

Timaeus by Plato. Desmond Lee translation, Penguin Classics, London, 1971.

When the Earth Nearly Died by D. S. Allan and J. B. Delair. Gateway Books, Bath, 1995.

When the Sky Fell by Rand Flem-Ath, published by Orion Books, London, 1996.

Index

aftershocks 170
Agassiz, Louis, 49–50, 52, 58
Ahmed, Hadji 136
Allan, D.S. 186, 191
alphabet 70
Altamira 75
Andes Mountains 105, 106
antler 69, 74, 75
Armstrong, H.L. 146
asteroid 184, 185–86
Athens 27, 29, 31, 33, 169
Atlantic Ocean 29, 149, 177
Australopithecine 11, 12, 17, 61
Aztec 152–154, 157
Aztlan 154

Baalbek 91–92
Baltinglass 114
Belousov, V.V. 165–166
Blavatsky, Helena Petrovna 156, 159, 165
BSM (Big Sweaty Men) Theory 88, 94
bulls 41–43

Cabrera, Paul Felix 144, 145, 146
Cabrera tablets 145
carbon dating 119, 164
Çatal Hüyük 85
cave art 58–59, 71, 75–78, 85
Ceres 185
chanting 95, 96, 98
Christianity 161
Churchward, James 158–160, 162, 163¬165
city states 25, 30, 31
Columbus, Christopher 34, 130
comet 184, 185
conquistadors 101, 153
Cuzco 110–113

Dashur 140
Dawson, Charles 61, 62–63
Delair, J.B. 186, 191
dinosaur 60, 145, 146, 147, 177
dinosaur footprints 147
Dorset Cursus 118

earthquake 33, 37, 169–172, 175, 180, 188, 189, 190
earthworks 117, 118
Einstein 125
Ellis, Ralph 138, 140, 141
Eratosthenes 132, 134
erratics 49–51, 56, 57, 190

farming 25, 32, 33, 67, 83, 192
flint 62
fossil 36–37, 50, 59, 60, 76, 106, 107, 147, 148, 155, 164, 166, 178, 179
Freemasonry 165

Gal Oya Dam Project 116
Gateway of the Sun 102, 103
glaciers 21–23, 49, 50, 55, 190, 191
global crust displacement, theory of 180
Great Pyramid (China) 116
Great Pyramid (Egypt) 67, 87, 88, 90, 115, 137–140, 141

Hapgood, Charles 125–127, 130, 132, 134–37, 160, 180–82
Herculaneum 173, 174
Heyerdahl, Thor 101
Homo erectus 12, 14
Homo habilis 11, 12, 14
Homo Neanderthalensis 12
Homo sapiens 12
Homo sapiens sapiens 12
Howard-Vyse, Richard 138
hunter-gatherer 24, 192
Huxley, Thomas 156

Ice Age 21, 24, 47, 48–59, 63, 64, 67, 72, 77, 83, 105, 116, 191–192
Ile de Gavr'inis 119
Inca 84, 110–113
Ipiutak 108
irrigation 32, 65, 67, 84, 118
Ishigoya Cave 82

Judaism 161

Kevkenes Dagh 113
Khufu 87, 88, 137, 138
King Midas 150
kings of Atlantis 30, 36, 39, 41–43, 150
Krakatoa 176

landslide 170
Library of Alexandria 130
Lyell, Charles (Sir) 50, 51

Machu Picchu 110, 111–113
Magellan, Ferdinand 123
Mallery, Alington H. 129, 130, 134
mammal 146
mammoth 75, 179–80
Maori 125
Marcellus 150
Marinatos, Spyridon 175
Mayan 157
meteor 177, 185
Mu 158–162, 163–65

Naacal 158, 160, 164, 165
Nineveh 67
Niven, William 141–144, 158, 160, 164
nomads 24, 70, 110

observatory 104
Oronteus Finaeus 134, 135
Osiris 161–162

Phoenician 122, 144
Piri Re'is 127–132, 134
Pitcairn Island 123
Plato 35, 44, 46, 64–68, 78–79, 82, 84, 86, 101, 120, 149, 150–151, 160, 169, 170, 175, 186–87
Pliny 172
Pompeii 173–74
Ponape 109, 167
Poseidon 37, 38, 40, 42
Posnansky, Arthur 103, 104, 113
prehistoric dam 116–117
prehistoric road 120
prehistoric water tank 120

Ptolemy 151
Ptolemy I 130

Qin Ling Shan mountains 116

Rapaiti 166
Richter scale 170
runic writing 72

scarab 124
Sclater, P.L. 155–156
Solon 26–29, 33, 35, 44, 46
solar system 9–10, 26, 53, 185, 186, 192
spirit cave 83
stone moving 65, 67, 86, 87–100, 101
Sun Temple 90, 101
supernova 186–88, 192

Tenochtitlan 152
Theosophical Society 165
Thoth 162
Tiahuanco 90–91, 101, 103–105, 107–108, 112–113, 137
tidal wave 170, 176, 180
Timagenes 150
Titicaca, Lake 90
tornado 188
trilobite 147, 166
trireme 30
tsunami 171
Tulupan 157

Uighur Empire 161
underground aqueducts 120

Vela theory 192
Vesuvius, Mount 173
volcanic island 172
volcano 53, 173, 176–77, 188